IN THE WAKE OF THE EMPRESS OF IRELAND

The Aftermath, painting by Yves Bérubé, oil (33¼in x 22in). (Collection of Guy D'Astous)

In the Wake of the Empress of Ireland

Rescue, Salvage and Investigations in the Summer of 1914

David Saint-Pierre

Salvaging SS *Chatham* in Florida in early 1910 after she grounded and started sinking. (Ralph S. Blydenburgh photo album, author's collection)

Front cover image: *The Aftermath*, painting by Yves Bérubé, oil (33¼in × 22in). (Collection of Guy D'Astous)
Back cover image: *To Those Lost*, painting by Yves Bérubé, oil (30in x 24in). (Collection of Guy D'Astous)

Originally published in French as *Dans le sillage de l'Empress of Ireland, Sauvetages, enquêtes et plongées à l'été 1914* by Éditions GID in 2023.
This English-language edition first published 2025.

The History Press, 97 St George's Place, Cheltenham, Gloucestershire, GL50 3QB
www.thehistorypress.co.uk

© David Saint-Pierre, 2023, 2025

The right of David Saint-Pierre to be identified as the Author of this work has been asserted in accordance with the Copyright, Designs and Patents Act 1988.

All rights reserved. No part of this book may be reprinted or reproduced or utilised in any form or by any electronic, mechanical or other means, now known or hereafter invented, including photocopying and recording, or in any information storage or retrieval system, without the permission in writing from the Publishers.

British Library Cataloguing in Publication Data. A catalogue record for this book is available from the British Library.

ISBN 978 1 80399 821 3

Typesetting and origination by The History Press. Printed in Turkey by IMAK

CONTENTS

Foreword		7
Preface		9
Introduction: Spring 1914		11
1	Late May and Early June 1914	17
2	The Yankee Salvage Association and the St Lawrence River, 1906–14	37
	RMS *Bavarian*	37
	SS *Mount Temple*	45
	USS *Yankee*	46
	RMS *Royal George*	54
3	Summer 1914	59
	June	59
	July	78
	August	104
	September	118
Conclusion: Autumn 1914		126
Appendix: Extra Images from the Album		128
Acknowledgements		140
Bibliography		141

To Those Lost, Painting by Yves Bérubé, oil (30in x 24in). (Collection of Guy D'Astous)

FOREWORD

Ralph Stratton Blydenburgh was my grandfather. I was 20 years old when he died in Wakefield, Rhode Island, at the age of 84. He was a quiet man, not much for going on about his life. I wish I had known more about him. I knew him as an owner of a country inn, but little more.

Thanks to David Saint Pierre, a Canadian maritime historian, I now know a lot more about him: my grandfather was an entrepreneur, photographer, seaman, ship salvager and patent holder. Not bad for a young man from Brooklyn! How did this new understanding of his life come to be? All because of a family scrapbook of 500 photos that found its way from a flea market to a famous online auction site, then to a historian always on the lookout for historical photos of ships.

I received a phone call that started, 'Would you, by any chance, be related to Ralph Stratton Blydenburgh?' And thus began my acquaintance with David, who told me the story of my grandfather and the *Empress of Ireland*. My wife and I travelled to Rimouski to meet David in person and to visit the museum dedicated to the *Empress of Ireland*. And now the museum will be the permanent home of my grandfather's photo album.

With his skills as a researcher and storyteller, David is enriching the history of the *Empress*. Thanks to my grandfather's photos, the story is even richer.

Jeffrey Blydenburgh, Winter Park, Florida, USA, October 2022

The bow of USS *Yankee* aground, seen from the bridge, 1908. (Ralph S. Blydenburgh photo album, author's collection)

PREFACE

In October 2021, my friend Sébastien Hudon, a historian of photography, spotted two photographs on an auction website. The two photos, incorrectly identified as 'Gaspe Lighthouse, *c*.1908', depicted scenes of men carrying equipment on the Pointe-au-Père Wharf with the lighthouse in the background.[1] Sébastien, knowing that old photographs of the Pointe-au-Père lighthouse interest me greatly, sent me the link to the auction. From the moment I saw the photos, I recognised the scene: some of the men carrying the equipment were wearing British Royal Navy uniforms and the equipment consisted of buoys and bundles of rope. There was no doubt in my mind that these pictures showed the men in charge of preparing the dives on the wreck of *Empress of Ireland*, carrying salvage equipment on the dock at Pointe-au-Père in June 1914. Only a few images of these operations had survived to this day, so these two photos were already exceptional!

There was more: the back of the two photos revealed traces of black paper still glued to the corners. These photos must have been peeled from an album! The seller of the photos, Sharon, was based in the United States and had other auctions online. Checking these other sales allowed me to see that several other photos seemed to have been taken from the same album, including five different photos showing the divers of 1914. Among these five photos, one was already known and confirmed that this was all related to the *Empress of Ireland* salvage operations. The discovery was already extraordinary, but if a whole album still existed, I could hardly imagine what it could contain and I wanted to acquire it, if possible.

I contacted Sharon immediately. She confirmed that the photos I was interested in were from a single album that contained several hundred photos of boats and divers and that she had 'just started to take it apart to sell all the photos separately'. My heart started racing and my hands got sweaty! What was in this album had the potential to be a major discovery for the maritime history of Canada and beyond. The saleswoman described the other photos as best she could and, as the conversation went on, she informed me that one of the pictures showed a 'skeleton' that divers were pulling out of the water. This single photograph, macabre but unique and unpublished, deserved to be saved, not squandered. If only out of respect for the victims of *Empress of Ireland*, it had to be preserved. I already knew enough, so I asked her the question: 'Would you agree to stop separating the album and would you sell me the whole thing outright if I made you a serious offer?' She accepted my offer and that's how I became the owner of this extraordinarily important photo album.

Once the sale was concluded, the album was to be sent to my home in Montreal, Quebec, Canada. We agreed to use the services of a well-known shipping

---

1 These two photos are reproduced on page 67 in this book. Note that throughout the book, I have chosen to use the French toponym of Pointe-au-Père, but up until the 1960s the English 'Father Point' was also often used.

company, whose reputation was well established. The next few days were spent nervously refreshing the tracking page for the parcel containing this precious historical artefact … until the update on the carrier's page stopped for a couple of weeks … and then was changed to 'Lost package – contact your shipper'. The horror! I won't go into the details of all the phone calls made, all the steps taken and all the emails sent, both by Sharon and by me. The carrier, every time its representatives were contacted, changed the story: one day they told us that the package was only late, nothing to worry about; the next day they told us that Ccustoms were holding it. Then they told us that it was lost in Canada, etc. There was no way to know the truth! This went on for six full weeks. The company launched an internal investigation to search for the package, which was unsuccessful, but they told me not to worry, that they 'could issue a refund for the shipping fees'! This was too much, I lost sleep and started making plans to go to company warehouses myself to meet people who could help me find the package. Then, shortly before Christmas, I get this email from Sharon with this opening line: 'DAVID!!! CHRISTMAS MIRACLE!!!! Your package has been discovered!!!!!' She had just hung up with an employee of the shipping company who had the package in her hands. The label had been ripped off by accident in Montreal and the package, without an address, had been returned to an American warehouse where all lost packages are opened, one by one, to try to identify the sender or the recipient. Luckily, Sharon had put her business card inside the box, which made it possible to contact her. Without it, the album would have been thrown in the bin!

This photo album, once in my hands, turned out to be as amazing as I expected, and more! It contains more than 520 original photographs, taken between 1908 and 1917. All the photos document the operations of the Yankee Salvage Association, a New York-based salvage and wrecking company. Finding a photo of divers or wreck salvage from the early twentieth century is a rare event in itself, but finding several hundred is once in a lifetime! Among these photos, fifty-six document the salvage diving operations over *Empress of Ireland* in the summer of 1914. For more than 100 years, only a few of them were known to have been printed as souvenir postcards at the time of the sinking. However, the other photos in the album are also of great interest and many were also taken in the St Lawrence River and elsewhere in Canada. The months following the acquisition of the album were devoted to research and writing, as a whole field of maritime history opened up before me.

In the following pages, some of the results of this research are presented to the reader through an unpublished story: how did workers and engineers from New York end up spending the summer of 1914 in Rimouski? Why them and what did they do during all these months on the wreck of *Empress of Ireland*? What happened on the shores of the St Lawrence during this season of 1914, which saw a part of the world engaged in a terrible war? Through hundreds of unpublished photos, most of which are taken from the album acquired in 2021, I take you on a journey of discovery of a little-known part of our maritime history.

David Saint-Pierre,
Montreal, Canada, 2025

INTRODUCTION: SPRING 1914

The year 1914 began like the previous ones along the St Lawrence River. The usual religious ephemera dominated the front pages of local Quebec newspapers. Of course, some more worrying news marked the first days of the year: the lack of water in Montreal, caused by major aqueduct breaks, led to health concerns and prevented firefighters from doing their job at the height of the fire season. In Ottawa and Quebec City, the troubles caused by high inflation were on the minds of politicians. In late 1913, Canada's Prime Minister, Robert Laird Borden, even gave a remarkable speech in Washington, in which he asserted that the whole world was facing this problem, and that North America was a late awakener to the effects of inflation. Ah, the innocence of the New World at the turn of the century! This speech essentially expressed the view that the economy had to rely on cooperation between all levels of government, and competition between European powers had to cease, to overcome the causes of the 'high cost of living' that was harming people in Europe and elsewhere. Little did anybody know that 1914 would be the year of an unprecedented global conflict.

As elsewhere in North America, Vaudeville shows were all the rage with the public. The biggest star of them all, and a crowd-pleaser wherever she went, was Quebec-born Eva Tanguay, who called herself the 'I don't care girl' after her signature song and her offhand demeanour on stage.[1] Movie theatres filled with enthusiastic fans lining up for a good laugh at the films of a new star actor, Charlie Chaplin. In less than a year, this London pantomime artist with the looks of a tramp appeared in more than thirty short comedy films and became a worldwide star practically overnight. The movie theatres were packed to the rafters despite the unusually hot, dry spring of 1914.

The month of May was so dry that forest fires ravaged several regions, including the lower Laurentians and Lake St John. Montreal found itself behind an ochre-yellow veil that obscured the city for several days. Other fires in the heights behind Saint-Roch-des-Aulnaies, in the Lower St Lawrence region, produced so much smoke that ships were forced to slow down on the river as visibility became very poor.

Immigration from Europe had reached a peak in recent years; in fact, 1913 had seen a record number of immigrants reach Canadian ports, with more than 400,000 people coming in.[2] Canada was a land of opportunity, and thousands of people were arriving to populate the western swathes of prairies and expand the

---

[1] She is often considered the first true mass-media star, and was by far the world's highest-paid entertainer at the peak of her career, around 1910. In Quebec, she performed in Montreal in 1909, but mostly inspired other artists, as in the Mardi Gras celebrations of February 1914 at Quebec City's Château Frontenac Hotel, when the highlight of the show was a man impersonating Tanguay! On her life and career, see: Andrew L. Erdman, *Queen of Vaudeville: The Story of Eva Tanguay*, Ithaca, Cornell University Press, 2012.

[2] '150 years of immigration to Canada', Statistics Canada, Government of Canada, 2016. (Consulted on the web, June 2024, at www150.statcan.gc.ca/n1/pub/11-630-x/11-630-x2016006-eng.htm.)

Captain H.G. Kendall presiding over a burial at sea on SS *Ruthenia*, April 1914. (*The Standard*, 16 May 1914)

ranks of this new country. Maritime news was a matter of great interest in the papers at a time when traffic on the St Lawrence was still growing steadily. The Port of Quebec was also enjoying a boom period, since the arrival in 1906 of the Canadian Pacific liners *Empress of Britain* and *Empress of Ireland*, which made it their regular terminal during the St Lawrence navigation season. New facilities to handle the thousands of immigrants passing through had just been inaugurated on Louise Jetty and the Breakwater Wharf. Large grain silos had been built in 1913 at the western end of the jetty, near where the St Charles River empties into the St Lawrence. At the beginning of May, the newspapers reported the appointment of a well-known local figure to the prestigious – and lucrative – position of harbourmaster in Quebec City: James Anderson Murray. This coveted job, which paid $4,000 a year, had just been entrusted to Captain Murray of the Canadian Pacific Railway's (CPR) Atlantic Steamship line. He had been captain of *Empress of Britain* from 1906 until 1913, when he was transferred to *Empress of Ireland*. His appointment as harbourmaster in Quebec City led to a game of musical chairs within the Canadian Pacific line, as the captain of SS *Ruthenia*, Henry George Kendall, was appointed captain of *Empress of Ireland* to replace Murray. Kendall arrived in Quebec City with *Ruthenia* after a crossing marked by the death of a passenger, who was buried at sea. In keeping with tradition, Kendall presided over this maritime funeral. As soon as *Ruthenia* entered port, Kendall boarded a train to Halifax to take command of RMS *Empress of Ireland*, which was then moored in that harbour, her winter terminal.

On 2 May, the very same day *Empress* departed Halifax with her new captain, Dr James Frederick Grant, a young medical graduate from McGill University in Montreal who had just been offered the position of surgeon on board *Empress of Ireland*, wrote a letter to his wife in British Columbia. He was embarking on his first ever Atlantic crossing and had just spent his first hours aboard *Empress*. His letter is tinged with some fears and apprehensions about the desirability of obtaining a position on a ship rather than in a hospital ashore: 'With the conditions I am offered in this position, I believe you will all be very proud to see me keep it, and working on board will add to my prestige and do you and myself more good in many ways.'[3]

---

3 Dr James Grant, letter to his wife dated 2 May 1914 and written on board RMS *Empress of Ireland*, by permission from the Grant family, collection Site historique maritime de la Pointe-au-Père (SHMP).

RMS *EMPRESS OF IRELAND*

Dimensions: 569.5ft length overall; 65.7ft breadth; 27.5ft mean draught

Tonnage: 14,191 gross registered tons; 26,715 tons displacement at mean draught

Builder: Fairfield Shipbuilding and Engineering, Govan, Glasgow (Hull No. 443)

Engines: Twin quadruple-expansion, 18,000hp

Speed: Service speed: 18 knots, max: 20.7 knots

Keel laid: 10 April 1905

Launched: 27 January 1906

Sea trials: 5 to 6 June 1906

Maiden voyage: Westbound: 29 June 1906 from Liverpool to Quebec; Eastbound: 12 July 1906 from Quebec to Liverpool

Safety features (in 1914):

10 watertight bulkheads

24 watertight doors (manually operated)

Marconi wireless apparatus (call sign MPL)

42 lifeboats, total capacity: 1,965 people; 16 seamless steel lifeboats under davits; 20 Engelhardt collapsible boats; 6 Berthon collapsible boats

2,212 lifebelts

24 life rings (half with floating emergency lights)

The first two-turbine-powered transatlantic ships, the Allan Line's RMS *Virginian* and RMS *Victorian*, were fast and comfortable twins of more than 10,000 tons, and at the end of 1904 confirmed that the Canadian mail contract would remain with this company. But competition wasn't far behind and by that time the Canadian Pacific Railway's decision was made: it had to build the best transatlantic ships for Canada and take the lead from the dominating Allan Steamship Line.[1]

The CPR awarded a contract to build two new passenger liners to the Fairfield Shipbuilding and Engineering Company of Govan, near Glasgow, Scotland. The Fairfield hull Nos 442 and 443 would be known to the public, starting in the autumn of 1905, as *Empress of Britain* and *Empress of Ireland* respectively.[2] At more than 14,000 tons and 570ft long, they would be the largest and finest steamships hitherto built for the Canadian service. The choice of naming one of the sister ships *Empress of Ireland*, even if the real title was never formally given by the British monarchy, was probably not unrelated to the fact that Sir Thomas Shaughnessy himself had Irish origins. The President of the Canadian Pacific Railway was thus paying a significant tribute to his ancestors' country, and this was certainly noted by the important Irish diaspora in North America. *Empress of Ireland* would be promised a glorious career and from then on would be a favourite of St Patrick's sons and daughters on both sides of the Atlantic! For eight years, she ran between Liverpool and Quebec City during the St Lawrence navigation season, and Liverpool and St John, New Brunswick, and Halifax in the winter.[3]

---

1 On the history of the Allan Line, one can refer to Thomas E. Appleton, *Ravenscrag: The Allan Royal Mail Line*, Toronto, McClelland and Stewart, 1974, or the more recent book in French, Annie Blondel-Loisel, *La compagnie maritime Allan: de l'Écosse au Canada au XIXe siècle*, Paris, L'Harmattan, 2009.
2 'Nouveaux steamers', *Le Soleil*, 13 October 1905.
3 Refer to the bibliography at the end of this book for a selection of works on the story of *Empress of Ireland*.

Empress of Ireland leaving Quebec on her maiden voyage eastbound, 12 July 1906. (Author's collection)

RMS *Calgarian* arriving in Quebec City for the first time. (Port of Quebec Archives)

1

LATE MAY AND EARLY JUNE 1914

In May 1914, for the first time since they were put into service in 1906, liners larger and more luxurious than *Empress of Ireland* and *Empress of Britain* began regular service on the St Lawrence. The Allan Line's RMS *Alsatian* and RMS *Calgarian* were the first ships to really challenge the leadership of the Canadian Pacific Railway's Atlantic *Empresses* since 1906. The competition between Canadian Pacific and the Allan Line, long a reality, had become rather friendly by early 1914. Although the transaction had not yet been publicly announced, Canadian Pacific had in fact acquired the Allan Line during 1909 and at the end of 1913 the two fleets were being prepared behind the scenes for a merger. In any case, officials of the Port Authority of Quebec, elected municipal officials and the media were jubilant at the arrival of the new Allan ships: Quebec City was becoming one of Canada's most important ports of immigration, and the St Lawrence waterway's reputation for safety added to its prestige. On Thursday evening, 28 May, RMS *Alsatian* was set to arrive in the Port of Quebec for her first visit to the city, a week after her sister RMS *Calgarian* had done the same. It was a busy day at the Port of Quebec. Several ships expected in the previous days were delayed by growlers, icebergs and icefields in the North Atlantic and only entered the harbour on the morning of the 28th. More than 4,500 passengers disembarked or boarded the liners, which followed one another all day long at the breakwater, the passenger transshipment dock at the end of Louise Jetty. Early in the morning, four liners disembarked their passengers: Canadian Northern's

A first-class passenger poses on the deck of RMS *Calgarian* during her maiden voyage eastbound from Quebec City, 24 May 1914. (Author's collection)

Three first-class passengers posing with two officers on *Calgarian*'s maiden voyage. (Author's collection)

RMS *Royal George*, Allan Line's *Corsican*, Canadian Pacific's *Mount Temple* and White Star Line's *Teutonic*. In the late morning, after a few hours at anchor out in the river, the Canadian Pacific liner RMS *Empress of Ireland* took back her place at the breakwater to begin preparations for her first departure of the summer season from Quebec City.[1] After a routine inspection of the life-saving appliances and watertight doors, the loading and stowage of luggage and boarding of passengers got under way, and the docks around the great liner were bustling with activity. The scheduled time to cast off for Liverpool was initially 3.30 p.m., but was later revised to 4.30 p.m., due to the docks having been so busy earlier in the day. The weather was beautiful and mild. On the boat deck, Ronald Ferguson, a 19-year-old wireless telegraph operator employed by the Marconi company, hadn't started his watch. He borrowed a deckchair and, lying back, watched the stevedores, sailors and officers of *Empress* busily load passenger baggage, the last of the cargo and provisions, and escort passengers aboard. In second class, the Salvation Army of Canada made up a strong contingent of 161 people, including its entire national Staff Band of twenty-nine musicians. Many of them added to these exciting moments of embarkation by taking up their instruments and playing a few pieces on the aft deck of *Empress of Ireland*.

---

1   The author published, in French, another book on **Empress of Ireland** with a more detailed account of her sinking: David Saint-Pierre, *Empress of Ireland, une histoire par l'image*, Quebec, GID.

The entrance to the Louise Basin in Quebec City on the morning of 28 May 1914. (Author's collection)

The Port of Quebec on the morning of 28 May 1914. RMS *Royal George* and *Corsican* are at the breakwater. (Author's collection)

In first class, eighty-seven people embarked, including several prominent business figures; the London acting couple Laurence Irving and Mabel Hackney; and Sir Henry Seton Karr, a former Member of the British Parliament, who was returning home from a hunting trip in Canada. In third class, 717 people boarded, many of them native Europeans now settled in North America, returning to visit family on the old continent.

At 4.35 p.m., the steam whistle on *Empress of Ireland*'s forward funnel sounded, announcing the ship's departure to the cheers of a large crowd on the docks. In all, including the crew, 1,477 people were aboard *Empress of Ireland*. None of them had any idea that their lives would be completely transformed – or ended abruptly – in less than ten hours.

It took *Empress of Ireland* just under eight hours to reach the Rimouski area, and then she proceeded to slow down on approach to Pointe-au-Père, east of Rimouski. About a mile and a half offshore, directly in line with the Pointe-au-Père Wharf and lighthouse, the Canadian Pacific liner stopped her engines to await the government pilot tender SS *Eureka*. At about 1.30 a.m., with *Eureka* alongside the liner, the St Lawrence river pilot Adélard Bernier, in command of *Empress* since she

These photos taken on 28 May 1914 at Quebec show passengers on the deck of *Empress of Ireland* awaiting departure, among them some Salvation Army members holding their instruments. (Salvation Army Heritage Centre, London, United Kingdom)

left Quebec City, disembarked on *Eureka*, handing over the helm to *Empress*' captain, Henry George Kendall.[2] At the same time, a few sacks of mail were unloaded to be landed, including the letters and postcards posted on board ship by the passengers since leaving Quebec. Once this operation was completed, *Empress* resumed her course towards Liverpool, moving a little farther offshore and down the river towards the Gulf of St Lawrence. Even though it was late May, the big ships were still passing south of Newfoundland on their way out of the Gulf of St Lawrence, rather than taking the more northerly route through the Strait of Belle Isle, as icebergs were still very much present in the North Atlantic this season.

Only a few minutes later, a lookout reported another ship in the vicinity. The weather was clear and the distance between the two vessels was estimated at about 8 miles. The other ship, the Norwegian collier SS *Storstad*, was sailing upriver, chartered by the Dominion Coal Company to deliver a full cargo of 10,000 tons of

---

2 For the sake of clarity and continuity, the time used is Pointe-au-Père, since it had been set and confirmed by wire telegraph at midnight from Montreal. *Empress of Ireland*'s and *Storstad*'s clocks showed different times.

The last known photo taken of *Empress of Ireland* leaving Quebec City, 4.35 p.m., 28 May 1914. (Musée Maritime du Québec)

coal from Sydney, Nova Scotia, to Montreal, Quebec. *Storstad* was a solid and massive ship. Built according to the Isherwood principle, which stipulates that the main hull steel braces be longitudinal, she was designed to withstand navigation in icy conditions. Commissioned in 1911, she was rather imposing with her 440ft-long hull and weight of 6,000 tons. A crew of forty was on board to ensure the smooth running of the ship.

Since *Storstad* had to approach Pointe-au-Père to pick up a St Lawrence pilot, she and *Empress of Ireland* would certainly have to pass each other at a short distance. While visibility was good, the officers of the watch of both ships planned their course and signalled their intentions to the other ship's crew using their ship's horn. Based on their position and course, the crews manoeuvred to cross the other ship's path green to green (starboard to starboard).[3] However, after a few moments during which the lookouts observed the other ship's movements and running lights, a thick fog bank rolled in from the south shore and moved rapidly to envelop the two ships, which lost sight of each other. On *Storstad*, officers on watch were convinced that just before *Empress* disappeared into

---

3   Ships, then as now, must have position lights to show their position at night. On the starboard (right) side of a ship is a green light and on the port (left) side, a red light. So, for example, if a ship turns in front of us at night, we will see one coloured light in succession, then both coloured lights at the same time (when the ship is directly facing us), then the light of the other colour.

On the morning of 29 May, the recovered bodies were transported to a shed on the wharf. Holding the stretcher are two Rimouski residents who had come to lend a hand, Abraham Lepage and jeweller Louis-Philippe Martin. (Site historique maritime de la Pointe-au-Père)

the fog, she made a turn and presented her red (port) side. For this reason, the officer in charge on *Storstad*'s bridge, Chief Officer Alfred Toftenes, was now convinced that *Empress* had changed her course and would cross red to red (port to port). Clearly, the crews of both ships had lost track of the other and officers on both sides were manoeuvring nervously. They slowed down, then ordered the engines to stop. Sound signals were exchanged by whistles and horns, but confusion reigned. On *Empress*, Kendall scanned the river from the starboard side of his bridge for any sign of the other ship. On *Storstad*, Alfred Toftenes, convinced that *Empress* now wanted to cross to port, ordered a turn to starboard to give the Canadian Pacific liner a little more room. Unfortunately, *Empress* was on the starboard instead, almost stopped and directly in front of him. When *Empress* finally came into view on *Storstad*, it was clear that a collision was imminent and inevitable. The order was sent to *Storstad*'s engine room to go full astern, but it was too late.

It was around two o'clock in the morning when *Storstad* rammed *Empress* amidships, penetrating more than 20ft deep into the liner's hull on the starboard side, before backing out immediately. The two ships lost sight of each other again, as *Storstad* retreated almost a mile to port. The breach in *Empress*' side was so immense that water entered the two large steam boiler rooms at a tremendous rate. The stricken liner listed rapidly, and when the dynamos were submerged, power failed and *Empress* was plunged into darkness. At the heart of the liner, in the middle of the night, passengers who were suddenly awakened had virtually no chance of finding their way to the upper decks, where the lifeboats were, with a deck layout still unfamiliar to them in this vast floating hotel which was listing. Despite their best efforts, the crew members were unable to fill the lifeboats and launch them.[4] Only a few starboard boats could be used, often because they had broken loose when *Empress* capsized and sank to the bottom of the river. In just fourteen minutes, in the middle of the night, *Empress* disappeared completely from the surface of the St Lawrence.

Empress' senior Marconi operator, Ronald Ferguson, had just enough time to send out an SOS, which was received by William Whiteside, the senior operator at the Marconi station in Pointe-au-Père. From there, *Eureka* was immediately dispatched to the scene. A few minutes later, the signal was also given to SS *Lady Evelyn*, the government mail tender stationed at Rimouski, to leave that port quickly and go to the rescue of *Empress*.

When these two boats arrived on the scene, forty-five minutes and one hour later respectively, they could not do much for the shipwrecked. Of the 1,477 people on board when the liner left Quebec City the day before, only 465 had survived. More than half of them were members of the crew. The disaster was immense. The survivors, most of whom were injured and freezing cold, were first rescued and taken on board by *Storstad*, whose crew members did everything in their power to help them. *Lady Evelyn* and *Eureka* later took these survivors off *Storstad* to bring them ashore at the Rimouski dock. They made a few more trips during the night, but only to find dead bodies, broken boats and debris on the surface of the river.

In the small French Canadian town of Rimouski, on the shore of the St Lawrence, daily life was disrupted by the events. From the moment the distress messages transmitted by the big liner were received at the Marconi station in Pointe-au-Père, around two o'clock in the morning, the news spread. John McWilliams, superintendent of the Pointe-au-Père pilot station and agent for the telegraph company, had already wired about the disaster to the Canadian Pacific Railway authorities in Montreal and the Intercolonial Railway stations. He had also telephoned a few people in Rimouski to help prepare for rescue operations.

When the two rescue ships, *Eureka* and *Lady Evelyn*, docked in Rimouski with hundreds of shocked and water-soaked, half-naked survivors and around 200 bodies, some Rimouski residents were already on the pier to witness the sad spectacle and to lend a hand, however they could. In the early morning, the rest of the town of 3,500 inhabitants was informed of the tragedy that had just taken place nearby by a special 'extra' edition of the local newspaper *Le Progrès du Golfe* that had been printed during the night with the first available news.

All rescue operations had to be organised simultaneously in the early hours of the morning, and the events mobilised the population and authorities to the maximum capacity of the small town. Some Rimouski residents, rich and poor alike, started flocking to the port with clothes, food and alcohol to comfort the poor souls who had just survived this horrendous tragedy. Horse-drawn carriages and automobiles crowded the quayside to transport survivors to the town centre, just a few kilometres away. Many of them were injured and naked, or in their soaked night clothes; they were cared for by the Sisters of Mercy Hospice, among other institutions, and stores opened their doors to distribute clothing and blankets.

For want of better space, the bodies of those who had been fished out of the water or those who had not survived the night were piled up on the floor of a small

---

4   Because of the list, port-side boats simply could not be lowered.

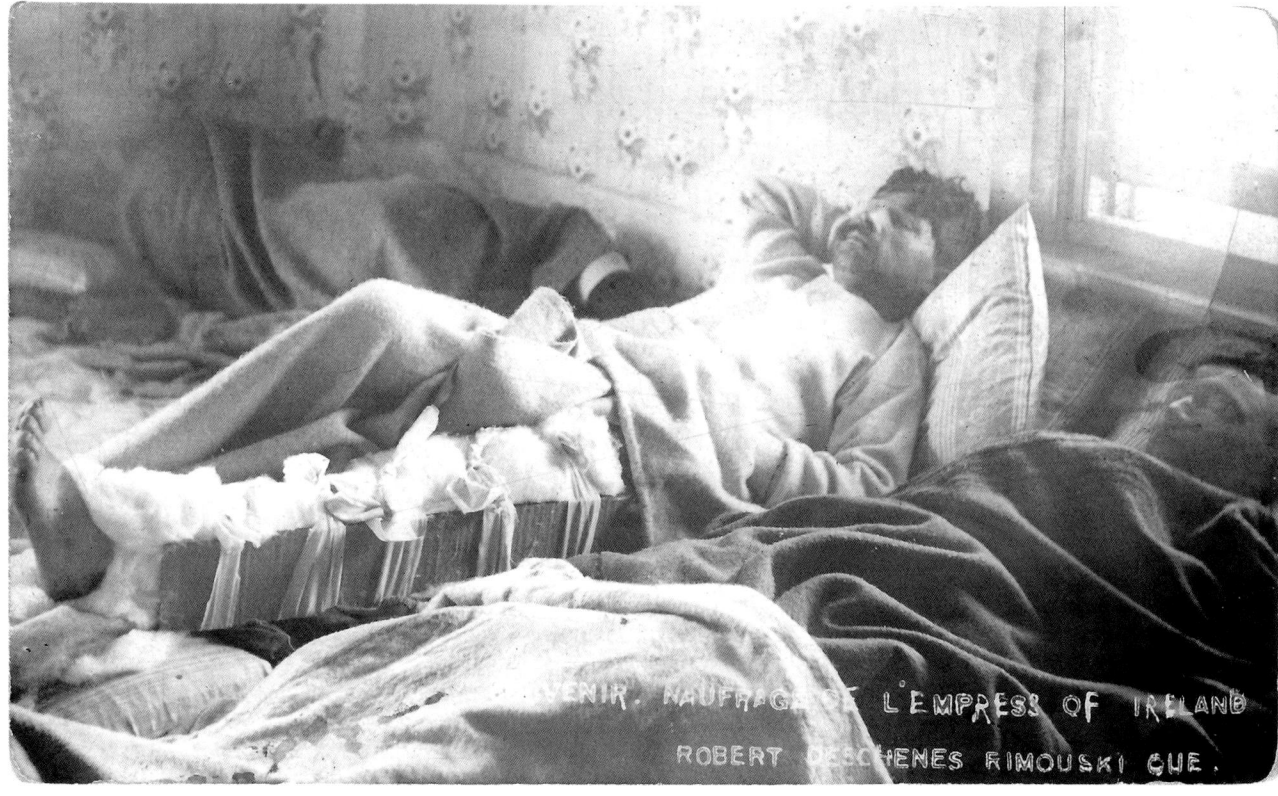

Three injured survivors are treated at the home of Ubald Lavoie, manager at the Port of Rimouski. (Site historique maritime de la Pointe-au-Père)

coal shed at the entrance to the wharf. All the town's coffins were hastily assembled, but their number was far from sufficient. Workmen and citizen volunteers were called in to prepare makeshift coffins from pine planks, but the town's resources were too limited for the number of bodies recovered during the night. The decision was made to send them to Quebec City. For the remainder of the summer, when bodies were recovered, embalming and other funeral arrangements were entrusted to Joseph Lepage, a local Rimouski undertaker working with the assistance of Canadian Pacific Railway police officers.

The survivors, most of them in shock, injured and having just lost everything they had brought with them, were taken care of in different places in Rimouski. Survivors were hurried over to hotels, and some of them were taken to general stores, which opened their doors very early in the morning to distribute clothing and basic necessities. Walter Erzinger, a second-class passenger who had been travelling from Winnipeg to Switzerland to visit family, was brought to the home of Georges-Alfred Marois, a Rimouski entrepreneur who, like so many other residents, had rushed to the wharf to lend a hand.[5]

---

5   Mr Erzinger made it to Quebec City at the end of 29 May with the other survivors, but even though he had only spent a few hours with the Marois family, he was forever grateful to them for their generosity. He and Mrs Marois maintained a written correspondence up until the 1970s, when Mrs Marois passed away.

A steerage survivor with bandaged head is telling his story to D.W. Sheehan, a Great North Western Telegraph Company representative, at Rimouski train station, 29 May 1914. (Author's collection)

During that whole day, the Canadian Pacific Railway authorities were busy making arrangements to take care of the survivors, reunite them with relatives or caretakers, or get them to their destination. Rimouski train station served as a temporary headquarters, and it is here that survivors were brought at midday to prepare for their journey back to Quebec City and Montreal.

First-class passenger Murton Darling later recalled:

News was circulated that the CPR (Canadian Pacific Railway), having got together a train, we were to go to the depot at noon, at which time the heat was very great. None of us knew how many had got through, we had hardly known each other […] in those few hours aboard ship. So that as odd groups dribbled into the depot, nearly all accompanied by their kind host, faces were carefully examined for possible recognition. Occasionally a cry as some portion of a broken family might discover a relative, perhaps to learn that only they remained of a family. […]

The hot hours of waiting dragged on, but a group of women set up a table in the depot cutting loaves and meat, cake and pies, with distribution to all. Casualties with bandaged heads, bound limbs were lifted aboard the train, and here again the kind folk of Rimouski provided their own pillows and blankets to ease the train journey for these sufferers.

Finally, just as it seemed we should really get away, a grizzled old farmer arrived in his cart in a cloud of dust, his horse a lather of sweat in the broiling sun – he had brought his morning's milk from his distant, farm, two large cans, with odd cups and a jug. He anxiously handed this to anyone within reach.[6]

At the end of the afternoon, those who were able to make the trip were sent to Quebec City by the Intercolonial train, as it was clear that despite the tremendous efforts made by the people of Rimouski, the town was too small to take care of the 465 survivors of the disaster. Only a few dozen survivors who were too ill to move were left in Rimouski for a few more days.[7]

On 30 May, the Cunard liner *Ausonia* was sailing to England with Salvation Army members en route to the organisation's Fourth International Congress in London. Of the 161 Salvation Army members aboard *Empress of*

---

6   Captain Murton Daniel Addison Darling, 'Rimouski Calls for Help, Her Citizens Aided Saanich Man Years Ago', *Saanich Peninsula and Gulf Islands Review*, Sidney, Vancouver Island, BC, Wednesday, 7 June 1950, p.4.
7   Precise numbers are extremely hard to establish due to a lack of available reliable sources. Research continues on these aspects of the aftermath.

An Engelhardt collapsible boat from *Empress of Ireland* adrift near the site of the disaster, photographed on 30 May. (Salvation Army Archives of Canada and Bermuda)

Ireland on 28 May, 133 lost their lives in the tragedy. The twenty-nine-member Canadian Staff Band, members of which had performed a few pieces on departure from Quebec City and offered free concerts on board on the evening of 28 May, was decimated. As *Ausonia* passed over the wreck, she slowed down to hold a brief ceremony in honour of the victims and a little further on she passed a broken and drifting lifeboat from *Empress of Ireland*. This photo of the overturned boat was taken from the deck of *Ausonia* by a member of the Salvation Army Band from Peterborough, Ontario. One can only imagine his feelings as he took this picture, a tangible reminder of the tragic loss of dozens of his colleagues the day before.

That same day, CGS (Canadian Government Ship) *Lady Grey* arrived at Rimouski Wharf to take on board a sad cargo: nearly 200 bodies of the victims of the shipwreck, in coffins and pine boxes. Rimouski's capacities were stretched to the limit, and Quebec City was in a better position to organise embalming and preparation of the bodies for identification. It was therefore decided to take the bodies recovered to date back to the Port of Quebec on *Lady Grey*. HMS *Essex*, a Royal Navy Monmouth-class armoured cruiser passing through the St Lawrence, was anchored off Rimouski, and her commander met up with the captain of *Lady Grey* to offer him an escort to Quebec. At around 4 p.m. on the same day, *Lady Grey* cast off and steamed towards Quebec, loaded with coffins. Leaving Rimouski for Quebec City, the two ships in the funeral procession made a detour over the wreck of *Empress of Ireland* for a short ceremony aboard *Essex*.

Only one civilian passenger was aboard *Lady Grey* for this funeral voyage: Salvation Army Captain Gideon Miller. Two days earlier, Captain Miller had been in Quebec City to bid farewell to his comrades en route to

Lady Grey loaded with coffins, photographed from the deck of HMS *Essex*, 31 May 1914. (Author's collection)

the London Congress. Although not taking part in the voyage himself, he had been privileged to come aboard for a few hours to participate in a short, friendly get-together with a few other Salvation Army officers, in the stateroom of Commissioner David Mathias Rees. Miller disembarked from *Empress of Ireland* at the sound of the departure bugle and the usual cry, 'All ashore that's going ashore', inviting people not sailing to leave the ship. He returned to Montreal by the 11 p.m. train. On his arrival at around 6 a.m. on Friday, 29 May, he heard the terrible news of the sinking and immediately set off for Rimouski to try to identify the victims. In Rimouski, he met Captain Kendall at the coroner's inquest, set up only a few hours after the sinking in a school house near the wharf. Kendall had asked him how many Salvation Army personnel had been lost, and Miller had to tell a shocked Kendall that only about twenty survivors from the contingent had been located.

When *Lady Grey* and HMS *Essex* left the site of the disaster to resume the route upriver to Quebec City, a barrage of dark clouds suddenly appeared to the west, and Miller witnessed a frightening thunderstorm that passed quickly to give way to a full rainbow forming an arch over the river and under which the convoy had to pass.

Upon arrival in Quebec City on 31 May, *Lady Grey* was awaited by an estimated 10,000 people, who crowded the entrance to Pier 27 to witness the scene. In front of many photographers and 'moving picture men', the coffins were

▲ At the coroner's inquest table, the day after the sinking. Coroner Dr Josué Pineault is in the middle, looking at his notes. (Pat Whitehead)

◄ Memorial ceremony over *Empress of Ireland* on the deck of HMS *Essex*, 30 May 1914. (*Daily Mirror*)

unloaded one by one by sailors from *Essex* and placed in the temporary morgue set up in the passenger ships' baggage shed on the wharf.[8] Just a few days prior, the people now lying in coffins for identification had been in that same room, getting their baggage labelled and processed by Canadian Pacific Railway employees, and were excited to see *Empress of Ireland*, moored a few feet away and towering over the shed.

For a few days, this makeshift morgue was the scene of tragic situations when relatives of the victims found the remains of a loved one, or when they did not find them after careful examination of the bodies displayed. Only cries and sobs broke the silence of the hangar from time to time. The Salvation Army was able to identify and claim twenty-two of their own, and arrangements were quickly made to return these bodies to Toronto. In other cases, two different families sometimes claimed the same body, and in one such tragic case it took the intervention of a Quebec City judge to settle a dispute over the body of a child.

Storstad, with her bow damaged by the collision, slowly made her way upriver to Montreal, escorted by the salvage tug *Lord Strathcona* and under the command of local river pilot Nault. All along the river, crowds awaited the collier to see the damage to her bow. Off Quebec City, the captain of the river ferry even went as far as to cruise around the collier so that his passengers could get a

---

8   The entire account of these events is taken from Captain Gideon Miller's unpublished diary for the year 1914, which I was given access to by the late David Creighton, himself a descendant of a victim of the *Empress of Ireland* disaster. Miller would later be responsible for the design of the memorial headstone for the victims from the Salvation Army, installed in Mount Pleasant Cemetery in Toronto.

The coffins installed for the identification of the bodies in the temporary morgue in the baggage shed on Pier 27 on the breakwater in the Port of Quebec, Sunday, 31 May 1914. (Musée de la Civilisation, donation of the family of Cécile and Robert Lépine)

A young woman is being supported and comforted after failing to find the body of her mother in the temporary morgue on Pier 27. (Author's collection)

HMS ESSEX

The Royal Navy ship HMS *Essex* was an 8,000-ton cruiser built in 1901 and placed under the command of Hugh D.R. Watson in January 1914. Her routine cruising mission took her during the first months of 1914 to the West Indies and to the Gulf of St Lawrence, along the coast of Newfoundland, in May 1914. The ship was already scheduled to be in Quebec City for part of the month of June, as she was needed to bring the Governor General of Canada, His Royal Highness Prince Arthur, Duke of Connaught, to Newfoundland for a formal visit in July.[1] But when the news of the sinking of *Empress of Ireland* was received by wireless telegraph on the morning of 29 May, she was ordered by the Admiralty to proceed to the scene and render assistance in the rescue operations. As luck would have it, the ship carried a team of divers and the very latest high-quality diving equipment, including underwater telephones and underwater electric lamps. HMS *Essex* would eventually spend more time than initially planned in the St Lawrence, before heading out to Newfoundland and being mobilised when war was declared on 4 August 1914.

▲ HMS *Essex*. (Author's collection)

▶ A commemorative postcard of HMS *Essex* missions from 1914 to 1916. For June 1914, only the name 'Quebec' is mentioned, while the ship assisted the salvage operations. (Author's collection)

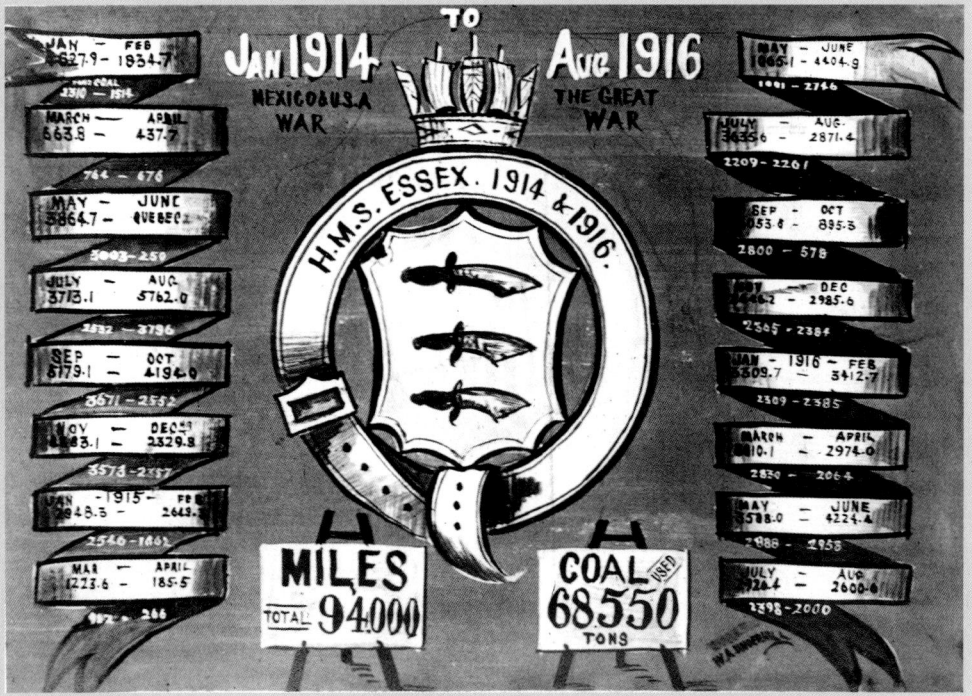

---

1 Incidentally, when the Duke of Connaught came to Canada to become Governor General in October 1911, he crossed the Atlantic with his family on *Empress of Ireland*. Some of the first-class staterooms of *Empress* had been refitted for the occasion, and they were renamed the Duke and Duchess cabins. When *Empress* left Liverpool with the duke on board, she flew the Royal Standard, one of very few occasions when a merchant vessel was awarded such a privilege (Derek Grout, op. cit., p.67).

A photo of *Storstad* taken by a passenger of SS *Hannover* in Montreal. (Author's collection)

good view of the ship, almost causing a collision himself.[9] After stops in Lévis and Trois-Rivières, she finally arrived in Montreal, awaited by a large crowd that had gathered on the docks to witness the scene. She slowly approached Hochelaga Pier, where the Dominion Coal Company had coal storage facilities, to unload her cargo. Among the crowd, a passenger disembarking from SS *Hannover* on 30 May took a photograph of the damaged ship, thirty minutes after *Storstad*'s arrival. *Hannover* had left Rotterdam on 19 May and was about 50 miles downriver from Pointe-au-Père when *Empress* sank on the night of 29 May. William Whiteside, the Marconi operator at Pointe-au-Père, had called by wireless for *Hannover* to come to the rescue of *Empress*, but *Hannover* arrived on the scene as the sun was rising and nothing more could be done for the victims. This passenger wrote on the back of the photo, 'Although we were only 30 minutes away, when we arrived at the scene, only bodies and debris

---

9   This incident was reported as being *Storstad*'s fault in some newspapers, only to be rectified by the river pilot himself in the 16 July edition of the Montreal French daily paper *La Presse*. (D. Nault, 'À propos du Storstad', *La Presse*, Montreal, 16 July 1914, p.3.)

were floating on the surface.'¹⁰ When the first reports of the accident were transmitted from Pointe-au-Père, some of the accounts during the night had confused *Storstad* with *Hannover* and a few European newspapers had erroneously announced that the collision had occurred with *Hannover*.

Above the wreck, a small temporary buoy topped by a British flag was installed, anchored by a harpoon, on the morning of 30 May by the crew of *Lady Evelyn*, commanded by Captain Jean-Baptiste Pouliot. It was not difficult to locate the wreck because air bubbles and oil were still escaping from the hull, lying on the bottom of the river. A much larger buoy was installed later that day by Captain Gagnon of CGS *Druid*, about 100ft north of the wreck. This one was green with a flashing white gas-powered light and identified by large letters spelling 'wreck' in white paint. This large buoy was moored using a coordinate point fixed with landmarks on the shore: Sainte-Flavie church belltower, Sainte-Luce church and the Pointe-au-Père lighthouse.¹¹

At the site of the disaster, the first few days were busy with the visit of one ship after another to pay tribute to the lost liner. On 31 May, around noon, the manager of the private Anticosti Island, Georges-Martin Zédé, aboard *Savoy* (the personal steam yacht of Mr Henri Menier, owner of the island), made a detour on his way from Quebec City to Anticosti to pay his respects to the victims of the *Empress* disaster. While near the buoy set up the day before, he took some photos of a collier and *Lady Evelyn*, with flags at half-mast, which also passed by the scene. When *Savoy* resumed her course at about 3 p.m., she came across a lifeboat from *Empress of Ireland*, which was overturned and adrift.

A large 'wreck' buoy was installed on 30 May near the sunken *Empress*. (Ralph S. Blydenburgh photo album, author's collection)

As soon as the news of *Empress*' sinking spread worldwide, steps were taken to organise dives on the wreck. In the St Lawrence, the Quebec Salvage and Wrecking Co. was by contract the official first responder for stranded or distressed ships. However, it was not the

---

10 Photograph from the author's private collection.
11 This position would eventually be used to rediscover the wreck during the summer of 1964, by a team of amateur divers from Gatineau, Quebec, helped by a Rimouski crew including M. Donald Tremblay, a professor at the Marine Institute, and entrepreneur M. Aubert Brillant.

Photos of the ships at the site of the sinking of *Empress of Ireland*, Sunday, 31 May 1914. (BANQ, 03Q, P186, S2, D1-13)

only company that could participate in salvage operations and, faced with the prospect of such an important diving operation, several big names in the Canadian maritime world petitioned the government to obtain the lucrative contracts that were sure to be awarded to salvage the vessel or her cargo. On 2 June, the famous captain and explorer of the Arctic Joseph-Elzear Bernier sent a telegram to the Postmaster General, Louis-Philippe Pelletier, offering his services to recover the mailbags and valuables from the wreck. In his letter, he boasted that he could count on the services of two brothers, Edmond and Thomas Tremblay, experienced divers who had already made dives to these depths in the past.[12]

What Bernier did not know was that steps had already been taken by representatives of the Canadian Pacific and the Canadian Department of Marine and Fisheries to award the first diving contract to the Yankee Salvage Association of New York, which operated in Canada under the name Canadian Salvage Association, and which was led by engineer William Wallace Wotherspoon. The Canadian Pacific Railway, which had relinquished ownership of the *Empress* wreck to her underwriters, was anxious to have the bodies, the purser's safe and the silver bullion that she was carrying raised. In addition to this contract, the Postmaster General asked the Yankee Salvage Association to also bring back the mailbags, if possible, and they would be paid an extra fee depending on the value of what they returned. Representing the American salvage firm, Montreal businessman Lorne C. Webster had already been in contact with the Canadian Pacific Railway and the Postmaster General to arrange all contracts to be given to Wotherspoon's team.

When it became clear that the main contracts had already been awarded, some actors in the local salvage industry

---

12 National Archives of Canada, Postal Archives, Salvage of mails etc. from wreck of the 'Empress of Ireland', 1914–1916, RG 3-C-1, Volume 633, file 69265.

SS *Lord Strathcona*, the powerful tug of the Quebec Salvage and Wrecking Co. (Blydenburgh family)

protested vigorously. Albert John Lee, president of the Westmount, Quebec, Compressed Air Salvage Company, who had worked in the past with Wotherspoon, wrote to the Postmaster General on 12 June to complain formally: 'It does not seem hardly fair that work of this nature should be given to an outside firm while there are Canadians equally well equipped for the work and ready to go at a moment's notice.'[13] In fact, without taking anything away from the experience and capabilities of the Canadian companies, the reputation of William Wallace Wotherspoon and his men was well established and, at least since 1907, he had been the one called upon for the most difficult jobs and to save salvage operations that other companies had not been able to manage. The anticipated complexity of the salvage operations on *Empress of Ireland* made it obvious that the New York team should be mandated.

---

13 National Archives of Canada, Postal Archives, *ibid.*

Original broadside announcing the departure of *Bavarian* from Montreal on 3 November 1905, which would turn out to be her very last sailing. (Author's collection)

2

THE YANKEE SALVAGE ASSOCIATION AND THE ST LAWRENCE RIVER, 1906-14

In order to understand how the New York-based Yankee Salvage Association became so advantageously known, especially in the St Lawrence River, and who the people were who settled in Rimouski during the summer of 1914, it is necessary to go back a few years before the sinking of *Empress of Ireland.*

RMS *Bavarian*

The Allan Steamship line's RMS *Bavarian*, built in 1899 by William Denny and Brothers of Dumbarton, Scotland, was the first vessel over 10,000 tons to sail the St Lawrence River regularly. The Allan steamer, having left Montreal bound for Liverpool, ran hard aground on Wye Rock between Montmagny and Grosse Île on the St Lawrence on the night of 3–4 November 1905.[1] In the middle of a snowstorm, the river pilot, Paul Lachance, although very experienced, was unable to avoid the rock and his manoeuvres to try to get the liner out of her bad situation had the opposite effect and *Bavarian* found herself stuck and sitting on the rocks at high tide, her bottom plates torn open to the river waters.[2] Attempts to dislodge her with tugs were unsuccessful, and the ship, emptied of her passengers and cargo, was left in place with no hope of salvaging her. The bottom of her hull was ripped open over a good length, her holds were filled with water and she began to deteriorate in the middle of the St Lawrence waterway. Moreover, at this very late stage of the season, when the river was about to freeze over, any other attempt to refloat her was almost impossible and it became clear that the liner would spend at least the winter in this unfortunate position. CGS *Montcalm* sustained significant damage while attempting to tow the liner and the salvage support schooner *G.T.D.* was lost to a fire during yet another salvage attempt. Virtually every salvage technique known at the time was tried, to no avail, before *Bavarian* was finally abandoned to her fate in early winter.[3]

In the spring of 1906, several experts went to inspect the wreck, stranded and rusting away in plain sight along this busy seaway, but no one seemed to have a practical solution to offer. Robert Owen King, a Canadian engineer who was a McGill University graduate, heard about the case and went to inspect *Bavarian* himself in June. He thought that the compressed-air technique used

---

1 'Le Bavarian échoué', *La Patrie,* Saturday, 4 November 1905, p.24.
2 The pilot would receive a reprimand following an investigation into the circumstances of the grounding.
3 'À Québec', *La Presse,* 30 November 1905, p.3.

Bavarian stranded off Montmagny, winter 1905–06. (*The Standard*, 19 May 1906)

machine) factory.⁵ King had obtained a contract as a consulting engineer for this factory and the two men had developed a good relationship.

Wotherspoon had moved from Montreal in 1901 to work on the construction of the New York City Subway tunnels and had shown King how he used compressed air in their construction. By injecting pressurised air into reinforced, watertight wooden caissons (cofferdams), water could be driven out, allowing workers to work in them with dry feet.⁶ It was critical to measure the necessary pressure according to the depth, the quantity of water and the size of the compartments to be pressurised and to use a pressure only a little higher than that of the ambient water. It was with this demonstration in mind that Robert Owen King approached Wotherspoon to propose that he try the same technique to refloat *Bavarian*.

in the construction of the New York tunnels could be used to refloat the ship.⁴

Injecting compressed air into a ship to refloat her had already been tried before, but the enormous pressure exerted on the inside of the hull had caused some serious accidents. One of these accidents, which was fatal, occurred on SS *Mount Olivet*, grounded at Gibraltar in 1890, and this limited the use of this technique. But King's idea was a little different and involved the support of a friend he had met in Montreal a few years earlier, William Wallace Wotherspoon. Wotherspoon, an American civil engineer, had lived in Montreal between 1895 and 1901, when he worked as a manager of a 'linotype' (a newspaper composing and typesetting

In June 1906, King and Wotherspoon formed a company, King and Wotherspoon Salvage, and raised money for the operation. King raised money from Diamond Jim Brady, a flamboyant New York millionaire, and Wotherspoon raised money from his uncles, brothers Charles Fraser MacLean and John W. MacLean, prominent and politically active citizens in New York. In Quebec, other associates were approached and funding was found from, among others, Percival Molson, of the famous Molson Breweries family of Montreal.⁷

It took some time to organise the operation, raise the funds and collect the equipment. Above all, it was necessary to wait for the intense tunnel construction and maintenance season to end in New York in order to

---

4   On Robert Owen King, see the article by Galen Roger Perras, M. Bardon & R. Haycock, 'R.O. King: The Professional Odyssey of a Practical Canadian Engineer', *The Northern Mariner*, 18(2), 2008, pp.85–118, or the complete biography: Michael F. Bardon, Galen R. Perras, & J. Graham Lindsay, *Robert Owen King: Engineer, Scientist and Inventor*, self-published, Blurb.ca, 2023.

5   Little is known about the extent of Wotherpoon's ties to Montreal, but it appears that he periodically frequented the Quebec metropolis and maintained business ties there, at least from 1895 to 1927.

6   See box on W.W. Wotherspoon, on page 43.

7   'Le *Bavarian* renfloué', *Le Peuple de Montmagny*, Friday, 23 November 1906, p.3.

The *Bavarian* aground at Lévis after she was refloated by R.O. King and W.W. Wotherspoon. (*The Standard*, 8 December 1906)

assemble the team of workers that Wotherspoon wished to employ for this task. So it was not until November 1906 that another attempt to refloat *Bavarian* was made using King and Wotherspoon's technical scheme.

The plan was to use wooden cofferdams, as in the tunnels, to seal the bottom of the steamer from the inside, reinforce her upper structure with temporary frames and then inject compressed air into her holds to make her float and lift her. After a week of work, under difficult and unusual conditions for the workers involved in the operation, doubt set in on board and confidence waned. Even the team of sandhogs from New York, the tunnel workers that Wotherspoon had brought up to Quebec to work in the holds, began to doubt the success of the undertaking and to suffer from the cold and air pressure.[8] To reassure everyone and show that this new technique was safe, Charles F. MacLean, who was a New York State Supreme Court Justice, came personally with his wife to join his nephew in Quebec City and boarded *Bavarian* for the rest of the operations. After much effort, the compressors were activated and, on 16 November 1906, *Bavarian* was floating again and could be towed to Quebec.

Since the dry dock of the Davie shipyard was already occupied, the choice was made to ground the ship again

---

8   See the box about sandhogs on page 40.

THE 'SANDHOGS' OF NEW YORK

The first experiments in working underground, but especially underwater, with compressed air date from the first quarter of the nineteenth century. As early as 1843, a tunnel under the Thames River was inaugurated in London, built with the help of compressed air. These first experiments, in Europe and North America, allowed for the rapid development of technical and scientific knowledge about the effect of air-pressure changes on the human body. The ailments of workers who went underground and were subject to great changes in ambient air pressure were noted and studied. These included nosebleeds, headaches and feelings of drunkenness, but above all, what was commonly called 'the bends' – decompression sickness that could cause partial and often painful paralysis. All these effects were gradually better understood and controlled over the course of the nineteenth century.

In New York, the number and length of tunnels needed for the Subway and roads, especially under the East River and the Hudson River, required the hiring of a large number of workers willing to work underground in pressurised air. Very soon, they began to be called 'sand diggers', 'ground hogs' or 'sandhogs'. They recognised each other as a tight and strong community, through the development of an *esprit de corps* and a sense of identity associated with their particular trade. The risks inherent in the practice of this hard trade, the isolated and underground nature of the work and the character of the men who practised it further contributed to creating this strong team spirit. The result is that over the years, the sandhogs gained respect and became known in New York and beyond as the toughest of the tough: organised, independent, but also boisterous. Their stories, both positive and negative, often grabbed media attention and helped create a certain mystique about them and their trade.

One of these stories went around the world in 1905. Richard Creedon was working with three other sandhogs in a tunnel about 15ft below the bed of the East River. To prevent water from rising and to keep the earthen floor sufficiently watertight, a constant air pressure was maintained in the tunnel and the workers plugged any large gaps with mud. A hissing sound was heard, as if the air had begun to leak, and suddenly an explosion of compressed air occurred, throwing the sandhogs violently against the mud and wood wall … except for Richard Creedon, whom the pressure lifted and projected 50ft into the air! He passed through 8ft of mud and rocks, 25ft of water of the East River and then another 20ft in the air above the river, atop a geyser of water and pressurised air. Miraculously, he fell back into the water without a single injury and swam back to shore himself, declaring, 'I had a great view of the city up there!' Although he escaped unharmed from this unusual incident, Creedon became a symbol of the safety problems in the tunnels, bolstered public awareness of the consequences of 'tunnel sickness' and crystallised the reputation of the sandhogs. The incident was one of the cases that became instrumental in changing the regulations toward better protection for the workers and putting more safety procedures in place in the tunnels of New York. Creedon himself was recruited by Wotherspoon and participated in the work on *Bavarian* on the St Lawrence.[1]

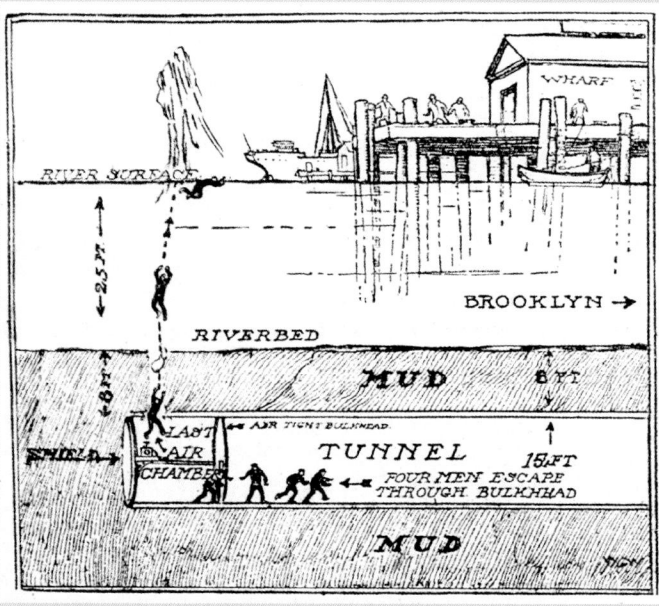

The incident of Richard Creedon as illustrated in *The Washington Times*, 28 March 1905.

---

1 James Morton Turner, 'Digging Tunnels, Building an Identity: Sandhogs in New York City, 1874–1906', *New York History*, Vol. 80, No. 1, January 1999, pp.29–70.

Bavarian aground at Lauzon, winter 1907. (Mariners' Museum)

The engineering team in charge of the refloating on the deck of *Bavarian*. The first on the left, first row, is Albert John Lee, and the last on the right in the same row is William W. Wotherspoon. (*Compressed Air Magazine*, January 1907)

right next to the shipyard in the mud of Indian Cove, while waiting for the fate of the former Allan ship to be decided.

The operation to refloat *Bavarian* cost $30,000, for a ship then valued at $500,000. Before King and Wotherspoon came up with their salvage proposal, more than $150,000 had already been spent on unsuccessful attempts.[9] Despite this, the operation did not pay off immediately for the two young engineers, as they had to come to an arrangement with Captain Lesslie of Kingston, Ontario, who had managed to get an exclusive contract for the salvage operation the previous year. Ultimately, the Allan Line had abandoned the ship to her insurers, and no one came forward to buy the damaged *Bavarian*, which remained stranded in Indian Cove for another year. In October 1907, almost two years after her last departure from Montreal, *Bavarian* finally broke in two off Lévis, rusted and abandoned. She was then dismantled and her steel sold for scrap, starting in the spring of 1908, but it took until August 1917 for the hulk to be finally completely removed.[10] Despite the steamship's undistinguished demise, the technical feat of her salvage greatly impressed, and several newspapers and specialised magazines around the world reported on it.[11]

Bavarian broken in half at Lauzon, autumn 1907. (Author's collection)

9   R.G. Skerrett, 'The *Bavarian* Floated by Air', *The American Marine Engineer*, Vol. 1, No. 12, December 1906, p.11.
10   Some of her furnishings found their way into Canadian homes: R.O. King himself kept a few souvenirs, and about half a dozen first-class dining saloon chairs are to this day preserved in different homes in Quebec. The author currently owns one of them. On the demise of the last traces of the wreck, see 'Nouvelles de Québec', *La Presse*, Montreal, 23 August 1917, p.7.
11   'Damage to the *Bavarian*', *International Marine Engineering*, Vol. XII, No. 12, December 1907, p.515.

W.W. WOTHERSPOON JR

Born on 6 June 1874 in New York, William Wallace Wotherspoon Jr was the only son of William Wallace Wotherspoon Sr and Helen MacLean. His father was a plasterer and landscape painter who studied fine art in Italy and was active in the Italian Revolution of 1848. W.W. Senior also developed a special technique for making plaster of Paris almost as hard as marble, a technique that would make him a renowned craftsman in New York. He would become known for his paintings of the New Hampshire mountains.

During his studies, W.W. Wotherspoon Jr became interested in mechanical printing technology, which is what drove him. He developed an improvement to the single-line machine, widely used in the newspaper printing industry, for which he received a patent in 1899. To circumvent American patents, Wotherspoon invested in Canada. At the end of the nineteenth century, he applied for letters patent to establish the Canadian Composing Company, a printing machine company based in Montreal. He was present in Montreal for a few years to supervise the work of the linotype machine manufacturing plant on Beaudry Street.

He then steered away from the printing industry and obtained a degree in civil engineering from New York University in 1898, while still living part of the time in Montreal. In 1901, he began working on tunnelling projects in New York City as the engineer in charge of sandhog work and participating in the dives and underground work himself.

Wotherspoon built himself a reputation as a marine expert after meeting Robert Owen King and the first successes in the world of ship salvage of their company, King and Wotherspoon Salvage. He used his knowledge (and contacts – he was distantly related to his famous namesake, United States Navy Admiral William Wallace Wotherspoon) to be promoted to the rank of lieutenant commander during the First World War.

Upon his return to civilian life, he resumed his maritime activities. From May to July 1920, he was again in the St Lawrence with the same men to participate in the refloating of CGS *Canadian Recruit*, near Tadoussac. In July 1922, he returned to the St Lawrence to participate in the refloating of SS *Orthia*, of the Donaldson Line.

Married in Greenwich, Connecticut, on 12 February 1925 to Theodosia Burr Clark, born on 11 February 1892, the couple had no children.

In 1927, the Montreal French daily paper *La Presse* reported that he held several shares in the Montreal Water & Power Co. that the Montreal city authorities wanted to buy.

Wotherspoon was apparently financially successful with his business endeavours and lived with Theodosia in a luxurious house on Staten Island, New York. He spoke with Admiral Edward Ellsberg about *Empress of Ireland* in preparation for Ellsberg's book, *Men Under the Sea*, published in 1939. The account he gave was very sensational and far from the truth.

According to family members, it seems that Wotherspoon may have suffered from a form of senility at an early age. Widowed and childless, he died at the home of a niece in Chicago on 20 March 1960. His body was buried in New York.

William Wallace Wotherspoon on a passport photo, 1921. (National Archives and Records Administration, Washington, DC, Volume 8, Special Series, New York)

The two illustrations of a US patent filed by King and Wotherspoon. (US Patent Office, Patent No. 851, 270, 23 April 1907, public domain)

In January 1907, immediately after the successful salvage of *Bavarian*, King and Wotherspoon filed a patent application describing their main salvage technique with the US and Canadian patent offices. They were granted inventors' patents in 1907, and from then on, their technique was protected by intellectual property rights. King and Wotherspoon were now key players in difficult ship rescues in the United States and Canada. Their invention, as described in the patent, was ultimately relatively simple: the interior of the damaged, water-filled ship was treated as one would when building a tunnel. That is, the water, instead of being pumped and scooped out, which is inefficient until the damage is repaired, was driven out by the superior force of compressed air. In other words, the air in the flooded area was pressurised to equal or slightly exceed the pressure exerted by the water itself. The air pressure had to be skilfully measured and calculated to represent approximately 1lb of pressure per 2.4ft of water in a grounded ship's compartment. In order to then 'lift' and refloat a ship, three major preliminary operations had to be carried out: the cargo and any excess weight of the ship had to be removed, the top of the flooded compartment had to be made watertight and the compartments around and above it had to be reinforced with wooden boxes, or caissons, to support the air pressure that would be injected. Finally, air compressors were installed on the surface and hoses directed the air into the compartments to be repaired. In order to make the necessary repairs, a watertight hatch with two doors was drilled into the deck above, to allow men to descend into the pressurised compartment to make repairs to the hull. The technique involved complex civil engineering, precise pressure and load distribution calculations, diving, shipbuilding and repair knowledge and technique, and the availability of manpower skilled in working in pressurised air conditions.

SS *Mount Temple*

After the success with *Bavarian*, King and Wotherspoon turned their attention to protecting their ideas, developing certain techniques and organising their company more formally. Wotherspoon would now concentrate entirely on salvage and refloating work. King, who was involved in some of his father's other ventures, remained active as a consulting engineer. Among the new investors was Lorne Campbell Webster, a prominent Quebec businessman who would remain a business partner of Wotherspoon's until the 1920s and who would later become the main representative of Wotherspoon's salvage company in Canada.[12]

In the early months of 1908, the crew of workers was also put in place, most of whom were the same sandhogs who had worked on the refloating of *Bavarian*. The patented technique was tested again, this time on the Canadian Pacific liner SS *Mount Temple*. On the night of 2 December 1907, the 8,700-ton ship, which was sailing from Antwerp, Belgium, to St John, New Brunswick, ran aground on the rocks of West Ironbound Island on the coast of Nova Scotia, pushed by sudden and violent snowstorms. The more than 600 passengers on board had to be disembarked on this isolated island and some of them spent the night in the cold, without shelter, before help could reach them.

---

12   At the beginning of the twentieth century, it was common practice to multiply corporate names and companies in order to maximise the sources of investment and spread the risks. One thus finds several names of companies, subsidiaries and branches, often associated with the same places of business and the same managers. For example, in the case of *Mount Temple*, it is under the name of North American Wrecking Company that the operations themselves were conducted, but it was always King and Wotherspoon who were behind it.

SS *Mount Temple* aground near West Ironbound Island, Nova Scotia. (Author's collection)

Exactly four years to the day after the successful refloating by Wotherspoon, on 15 April 1912, the same *Mount Temple*, repaired and recommissioned by the Canadian Pacific Railway, would become famous as one of the two liners to arrive at the scene of *Titanic*'s sinking, after receiving her distress messages by wireless telegraphy. When *Mount Temple* finally arrived in the vicinity of the tragedy, the Cunard liner *Carpathia*, which had just preceded her and had picked up the survivors, gave her the message to get back on course, as nothing more could be done and her help was no longer needed.

USS *Yankee*

The extraordinary progress made on *Bavarian* in the St Lawrence River and on *Mount Temple* in Nova Scotia was precisely what led a New York millionaire to call upon the services of King and Wotherspoon in the autumn of 1908. The Scottish-born philanthropist John Arbuckle, who had made his fortune in the international trade of coffee and sugar, wanted to invest in the maritime business towards the end of his life. He had bought an old ship to convert it into housing for the poor in New York Harbor, but now wanted to be more directly involved on the sea.[13] The grounding of the US Navy training cruiser USS *Yankee* on the rocks near New Bedford, Massachusetts, motivated Arbuckle to create a salvage company of his own that would use the patented technique of the two young engineers. He began by investing in the purchase of vessels to convert them into salvage boats with the latest equipment for diving and salvage operations. One of these ships was

Three attempts to refloat the ship had been made by the usual means in February 1908, before Wotherspoon succeeded with his compressed-air technique on 15 April 1908. Rescued from the rocks, the ship was brought to Halifax for repairs and returned to service less than a year later. Although the general public had already been very impressed in 1906, some people in the maritime trade had spread the rumour that the refloating of *Bavarian* had been a fluke due to the strength of the tide and could not be repeated. The successful refloating of SS *Mount Temple* put these doubters to rest and demonstrated unequivocally the extraordinary progress made by King and Wotherspoon.

---

13   Arbuckle is a fascinating and still largely unknown character. Throughout his life, he remained close to his humble origins and dedicated himself to improving the lot of ordinary people and workers. He became particularly well known for breaking the historic sugar cartels to bring down prices for the common people. Clayton A. Coppin, 'John Arbuckle: Entrepreneur, Trust Buster, Humanitarian', *The Freeman, Ideas on Liberty*, Vol. 40, No. 5, 1 May 1990, pp.192–96. Arbuckle would deserve a full biography.

▲ Philanthropist millionaire John Arbuckle. (Ralph S. Blydenburgh photo album, author's collection)

▶ USS *Yankee* aground in October 1908. (Ralph S. Blydenburgh photo album, author's collection)

The Yankee Salvage Association crew during the salvage operations of USS *Yankee*. In the front row towards the right, one can recognise, among others, the directors of the King and Wotherspoon Company: William Wallace Wotherspoon (fifth from right), Robert Owen King (fourth from right) and Ralph Stratton Blydenburgh (second from right). Among the divers is the Quebecer Thimolaüs Michaud. (Ralph S. Blydenburgh photo album, author's collection)

the famous SS *Roosevelt*, the same vessel made famous a few years earlier during Robert Peary's polar expedition.[14] Arbuckle had a specific plan in mind to test the capabilities of his new company and fleet.

In the heart of Buzzard's Bay, on the Atlantic coast of Massachusetts, on 23 September 1908, USS *Yankee* crashed heavily on Spindle Rock, very close to a lightship.[15] After unsuccessful attempts by several different companies, Arbuckle set up a subsidiary company that could use King and Wotherspoon's technology, the Yankee Salvage Association, in whose name he submitted his salvage bid. His offer was initially received with scepticism because, at this point, no one believed it possible that USS *Yankee* could be salvaged. Because the usual techniques – patches made of wood, cement poured into the cracks, pumps, tugs on the surface – had all failed and cost tens of thousands of dollars, the US Navy decided to give Arbuckle's scheme a try. With nothing left to lose, the navy awarded Arbuckle the contract anyway.

For more than a month, the Yankee Salvage team, led by King and Wotherspoon, worked hard to first undo the failed work of previous crews, before beginning to

---

14   For more on Peary's expedition to the Pole, you can read: Bruce B. Henderson, *True North: Peary, Cook and the Race to the Pole*, New York, W.W. Norton & Co., 2005.

15   'Triumph for the Modern Wreck, Floating the U.S. Cruiser Yankee', *New York Daily Tribune*, 13 December 1908, p.3.

install what was needed to refloat the ship, including cofferdams and mechanical compressors that could pump pressurised air inside the hull of the stricken cruiser.[16] The team was still the same, made up of sandhogs, divers and engineers. Late in the year 1908, a Quebecer from Lévis, where *Bavarian* ended up, participated in the work employed among the team of divers. The presence of this diver, Thimolaüs Michaud, was proof that Wotherspoon had kept some links with Canada, and the St Lawrence especially, since the refloating of *Bavarian*.

On 4 December 1908, *Yankee* was successfully refloated, and tugs began towing her into port. Meanwhile, a skeleton crew including *Yankee*'s own captain, Charles C. Marsh, and eight members of the Yankee Salvage Association, including Wotherspoon and Michaud, were still on board to ensure the air compressors were operating continuously. While *Yankee* was being towed, however, on the night of 4–5 December, a storm came up and the ship took on a bit of a starboard list, threatening to flood one of the compartments where the compressors were working. To add to the misery, one of the tugs snagged *Yankee* in the rough seas and water entered the starboard side through the portholes that had to be left open for the compressors to operate. As the ship began to take on water, Wotherspoon himself tried to go below deck, close the portholes and restart the flooded compressors. But seeing the water rise to his neck, he returned to the surface to avoid drowning. Michaud quickly donned his diving suit and descended into the sinking ship, risking his life in an attempt to close the portholes and keep the air compressors running while Wotherspoon, on the deck above, supplied him with air using a hand pump.[17] The operation failed, but everyone managed to save themselves in extremis from *Yankee*, which then sank again into deeper water.[18]

Wotherspoon's and Michaud's exploits were the subject of a letter of commendation from Captain Marsh to Admiral Evans of the US Navy, highlighting their heroic act in trying to save the ship and praising their courage

▲ Michaud, represented in the Quebec City daily *Le Soleil*, 22 December 1908.

◀ Thimolaüs Michaud trying to save *Yankee*, in an illustration published in *The Barbour County Index*, 13 January 1909. (Author's collection)

---

16   Henry Jay Case, 'The "Sand-Hogs" and the Ship', *Harper's Weekly*, Vol. LIII, No. 2727, New York, 27 March 1909, pp.6–7.
17   William W. Wotherspoon and Thimolaüs Michaud's exploits would be the subject of many articles in newspapers at the time. Just one example is 'Heroic Men on the Yankee', *The New York Times*, 13 December 1908, p.3.
18   'Nine Jump for Life as Salved Cruiser Yankee Goes to Bottom', *The Sunday Herald*, Boston, 6 December 1908, p.1.

▲ Two sandhogs atop a pipe used as an airtight lock that allowed them to descend into a compartment of the *Yankee* wreck, filled with compressed air, during a second refloating attempt. (Ralph S. Blydenburgh photo album, author's collection)

▶ Captain Marsh in the centre, accompanied by James McAllister (left) and William Wallace Wotherspoon at the beginning of the work. (Ralph S. Blydenburgh photo album, author's collection)

and dedication. In Quebec, the event was also covered by a few local newspapers, including the Quebec City daily paper *Le Soleil*, which ran two articles entitled 'The Canadians that Everyone Talk About' in its editions of 19 and 22 December 1908.

During the following years, other attempts were made to refloat USS *Yankee*, but without success. The ship had been damaged twice – first by the initial grounding, then by the collision and sinking – and her condition was too deteriorated to seal her up sufficiently to raise her. Then, in 1910–11, faced with the impossibility of refloating the ship, it was decided to carry out dives and operations to recover the cannon and some equipment from the wreck. Subsequently, the Yankee Salvage Association was tasked with breaking up what was left of the sunken ship so that the wreck would no longer interfere with shipping in this busy part of the bay. For the first time, the Yankee Salvage Association was given a contract that consisted mainly of deep-sea diving and salvaging items from a wreck. This experience would prove crucial for the future, especially when the company was selected to dive on *Empress of Ireland*. In the United States, the salvage of USS *Yankee*, even if it was only partially successful, was as important as that of RMS *Bavarian* for the reputation of the company, and William Wallace Wotherspoon in particular. From that moment on, the Yankee Salvage Association was established as one of the main expert companies in salvage and wreck diving in the United States and Canada.

Roosevelt beside a mast of the submerged USS *Yankee*, 1910. (Ralph S. Blydenburgh photo album, author's collection)

A huge bundle of ropes is loaded on *Roosevelt* to retrieve parts of *Yankee*. (Ralph S. Blydenburgh photo album, author's collection)

A diver climbing down a ladder attached to a mast of the submerged *Yankee*, while a winch lifts a box recovered from the wreck. (Ralph S. Blydenburgh photo album, author's collection)

Disassembled sections of *Yankee* are lifted on to *Roosevelt* to be sent for scrap. (Ralph S. Blydenburgh photo album, author's collection)

RALPH STRATTON BLYDENBURGH

The vast majority of the photographs reproduced in this book come from the photo album mentioned in the foreword, containing more than 500 unpublished photographs compiled by Ralph Stratton Blydenburgh, one of the directors of the King and Wotherspoon Company.

R.S. Blydenburgh, born on 29 July 1886 in Brooklyn, was the only son of Edgar R. Blydenburgh, a merchant, and Jane H. Oliver. He graduated from Brooklyn's Union Commercial High School in 1904, but we have little information on his subsequent academic training. He came from a wealthy family and was introduced to the maritime trades at an early age. As early as 1908, at the age of 22, he was a member of the refloating crew of USS *Yankee*. On the 1905 US federal census, Blydenburgh is listed as a 'clerk' in real estate, and on the 1910 census he is listed as employed in the sugar industry.[1] His employment connection with John Arbuckle in the sugar industry seems to have been how he first got into Arbuckle's other business endeavour: ship salvage.

Blydenburgh was named among the directors of the King and Wotherspoon as a secretary at this time and poses in some photographs, sometimes dressed for maritime work among the other men on the crew and sometimes dressed as a gentleman among the other company directors. Despite his executive duties, Blydenburgh was actively involved in technical work by 1908. In the years that followed, Blydenburgh participated directly in most of the company's diving and salvage operations, from Quebec to Mexico, Florida, the north-eastern United States and the Maritime provinces.

In the New York business directory, he was still listed as a director of King and Wotherspoon in 1918, but in practice, he had moved away from salvage operations. He married Marion van Wagenen Bailey in 1916, and with the United States' entrance into the war in 1917, King's and Wotherspoon's business slowed. Wotherspoon himself was in the US Navy in France, while R.O. King was in the British Army in Great Britain. Ralph Blydenburgh found a job with the Barber Steamship Line in New York as an agent in charge of acquisitions. He remained with the company until November 1927, when the branch he managed was abolished.

The following year, Ralph and Marion purchased the historic Larchwood Inn, built in 1831 in the heart of Wakefield, Rhode Island. They would continue to own this business, welcoming thousands of visitors from all classes of American society, until 1946.

Ralph Stratton Blydenburgh died on 19 August 1970, in Wakefield, Rhode Island.

Ralph Stratton Blydenburgh on a boat returning from Quebec to New York, Gulf of St Lawrence, autumn 1914. (Ralph S. Blydenburgh photo album, author's collection)

---

1   United States Federal Survey, 1910, Ward, Brooklyn, New York, District 0613, National Archives and Records Administration, College Park, Maryland, consulted on 10 April 2022 on Ancestry.com.

RMS *Royal George* stranded on the rocks, Sainte-Pétronille, Island of Orleans, Quebec. (Alain Franck)

RMS *Royal George*

On the St Lawrence, from that point on, the Yankee Salvage Association was often called upon for difficult contracts or those requiring a support team expertly trained in dangerous tasks. This is how the New York team once again landed in Quebec, on the Island of Orleans on the shores of the St Lawrence River, in November 1912, to kill two birds with one stone. SS *Gladstone* ran aground near the western tip of the island only a few days before the Canadian Northern Railway's RMS *Royal George* suffered the same fate off Sainte-Pétronille on 6 November.[19] With the help of George Duncan Davie's crew from the shipyard of the same name, the men under Wotherspoon's direction managed to dislodge first *Gladstone* then *Royal George*, which had been heavily damaged on the rocks. *Gladstone* was taken to the dry dock at Lévis to undergo some repairs to her hull. Because of this, the only dry dock large enough for these ships was already occupied when *Royal George* was dislodged. A way had to be found to repair the damage to *Royal George* so that she could return to sea, since wintering in Quebec City with her damaged hull could have meant that she might await the same sad fate as *Bavarian* a few years earlier.

It was this constraint that led Wotherspoon to propose another revolutionary idea: to transform the ship itself into a floating dry dock by using compressed air. Here, sandhogs, accustomed to working in highly pressurised air, descended into *Royal George*'s pressurised holds to perform hull repairs in the middle of the tidal basin in Quebec City Harbour. As the holds were filled with water, compressed air was pushed into the compartments and as the water was forced down, sandhogs made temporary repairs with boards and clay, which the compressed air helped hold in place. One can imagine the headaches,

---

19   'Steamship *Royal George* Runs Ashore at Point St Laurent', *The Québec Chronicle*, 7 November 1912, p.1.

Royal George during salvage operations, Sainte-Pétronille, Island of Orleans, Quebec, 1912. Note the absence of lifeboats, taken off to reduce weight. (Alain Franck)

Royal George being repaired while afloat in the Louise Basin, Port of Quebec. (Alain Franck)

earaches, nosebleeds and other effects produced by such extreme conditions for the sandhogs down below.

Once the air had permanently replaced the water in the temporarily repaired holds, wooden templates were prepared and cut to make steel plates strong enough for the ship to sail again. On the docks, the steel pieces were cut to fit the templates and bolt holes were drilled at strategic locations. The final step required sandhogs to work from inside the pressurised holds while specialised divers went underwater on the outside of the ship to attach the steel plates. This bold and daring idea was attempted successfully and *Royal George* was effectively repaired while afloat in the Louise Basin, without even going into dry dock. The Yankee Salvage Association once again achieved a feat that made headlines in specialised magazines all over the world and confirmed once again their reputation as the experts who did what others wouldn't dare.[20]

---

20 Robert G. Skerrett, 'The Salvage and Repair of the Steamship *"Royal George"'*, *Scientific American*, 26 July 1913, p.64.

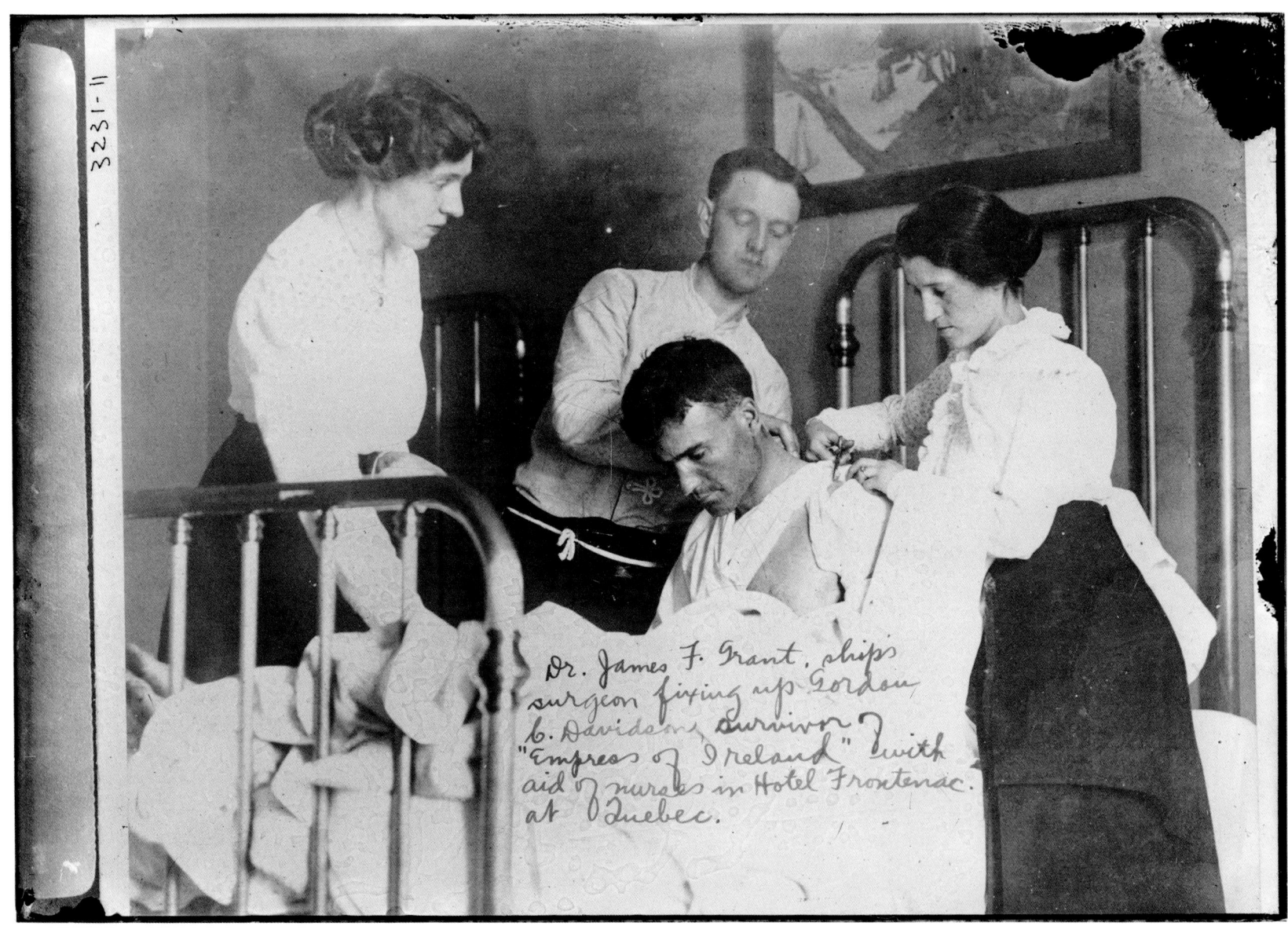

Empress of Ireland's surgeon, Dr James Grant, treating survivor Gordon Davidson at the Château Frontenac Hotel in Quebec City, 1 June 1914. He is still wearing the odd-fitting clothes he was given at Rimouski. (United States Library of Congress)

3

SUMMER 1914

John Arbuckle died in 1912, but the company he had co-founded, the Yankee Salvage Association, survived him with William Wallace Wotherspoon as its principal director. It was this company, with all the experience it had acquired over the previous years, that began operations on *Empress of Ireland* at the beginning of June 1914, when the authorities called on its services.

June

While the surviving passengers, shocked, exhausted and injured, were being treated in hotels and hospitals in Quebec City, the crew members were taken care of by the Canadian Pacific Railway Company. Some were sent back to their families in Great Britain on the next liners to leave Quebec. Others, however, were kept in Quebec to recover. The surviving officers were sent to the Viger Hotel in Montreal, another Canadian Pacific Railway establishment. Henry George Kendall, the captain of *Empress*, and the ship's surgeon, Dr James Grant, met there. Dr Grant, who had barely escaped the sinking ship by squeezing through a porthole on the side of the hull, injuring himself in the process, was widely praised for his tireless efforts to help the survivors in the hours following the sinking. He wrote a letter to his wife in British Columbia on Viger Hotel letterhead paper on 3 June:

All the surviving officers go to Québec today for the military funeral of our shipmates tomorrow. We have had new uniforms made for the funeral. I shall never use it afterwards. As soon as I get free here I shall come home to you, but my work among the survivors has given me a great deal of pleasure and I am still able to render assistance to those in need.[1]

In Rimouski, preparations were under way for the first dives to the wreck. Few people entertained any illusions about refloating *Empress of Ireland*. The ill-fated ship was huge, damaged to the point of sinking in just fourteen minutes, and came to rest on the bottom of the river at a depth of 140ft, some 4 nautical miles off the coast of Sainte-Luce-sur-Mer, on the south shore. The chances of bringing *Empress* back to the surface were virtually nil, but Canadian Pacific had to make sure all options were considered. This was the first mission given to the experts from the Yankee Salvage Association: ascertain the wreck's condition on the riverbed, her exact position and evaluate the possibility of refloating her.

On 5 June, divers from HMS *Essex* departed Quebec City for Rimouski to assist with the operations. Wotherspoon and two of his most trusted divers prepared a small quantity of equipment aboard CGS *Druid*, the Canadian Government buoy tender, for a first dive.

---

1 Letter from Dr Grant to his wife, by permission of the Grant family, collection of the Site historique maritime de la Pointe-au-Père.

The Allan Line's RMS *Alsatian* at the Breakwater Wharf in Quebec City, used as a floating hotel for survivors of the *Empress of Ireland* disaster, 1 June 1914. (Author's collection)

This was carried out on 7 June by an American diver, who descended along a chain released with a weight. Disoriented and in complete darkness, when the diver climbed back up, he said he did reach the wreck, but was uncertain of his exact location on it or of the liner's position and orientation on the bottom of the river. All he knew was that he bumped into a protruding part of the hull. Wotherspoon then noticed a dash of red paint on the diver's suit and deduced that the protruding part he had felt must have been the port-side bilge keel. This would indicate that *Empress* was resting on her starboard side. A second descent on the same day confirmed this intuition, with the diver walking on the hull away from the bilge keel and arriving on a white-painted section of the wreck: one of the upper decks! No doubt about it: *Empress* was lying on her right side, her bow pointing north-east. The rest of the day was spent installing a few guidelines on the wreck, to help with future dives.

It had been a difficult day. One of the divers slipped on the hull and almost drowned.[2] Better equipment and more rigorous preparation would be needed to continue the work. On 8 June, the winds were raging, and the dive attempts were cancelled. It was therefore decided to return to Quebec City and proceed with thorough planning of the diving operations, which would not resume until the necessary men and equipment had arrived. In Quebec City, the team would also take possession of *Marie-Josephine*, a schooner rigged for salvage diving and chartered by the Canadian Pacific Railway.

Wotherspoon and a few men were already in Quebec, but the rest of the team had to be assembled quickly. Arriving in Rimouski on the Intercolonial train late in the afternoon of 16 June 1914, Wotherspoon's crew for the operations over *Empress of Ireland* was made up of his best men, some of whom had been working with him

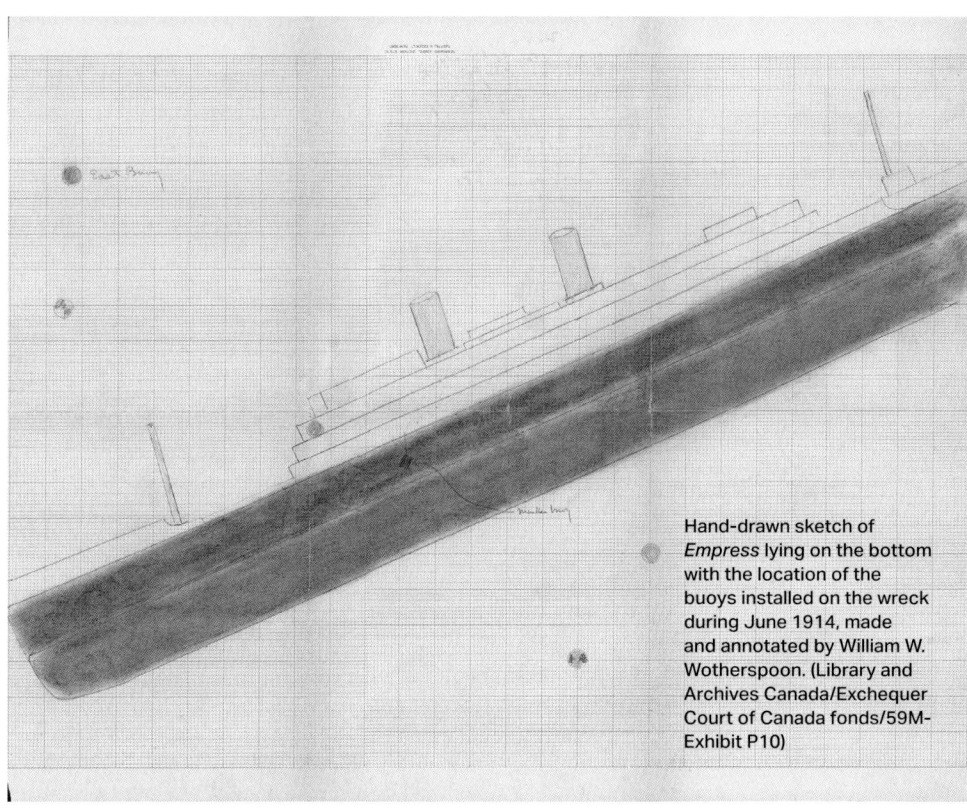

Hand-drawn sketch of *Empress* lying on the bottom with the location of the buoys installed on the wreck during June 1914, made and annotated by William W. Wotherspoon. (Library and Archives Canada/Exchequer Court of Canada fonds/59M-Exhibit P10)

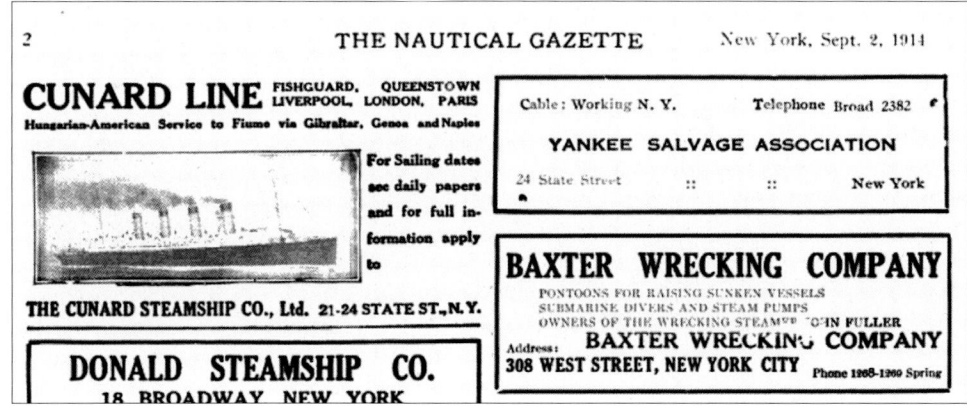

1914 advertisement for the Yankee Salvage Association. (*The Nautical Gazette*, 2 September 1914)

---
2 'L'un d'eux a été près de se noyer', *La Tribune*, Sherbrooke, 11 June 1914, p.3.

The Yankee Salvage Association 'wrecking crew' at Rimouski Wharf. (Ralph S. Blydenburgh photo album, author's collection)

for several years. On the same day, a smaller group of men from the Lévis-based Quebec Salvage and Wrecking Co. also arrived in Rimouski with equipment to begin the work. A 15ft-long by 5ft-diameter decompression chamber was shipped from Montreal and installed on the schooner *Marie-Josephine*. An entire wagon of the Intercolonial train arrived in Rimouski loaded with equipment, and another one was brought in carrying ice, to preserve the bodies that would be recovered from the wreck.

This team, made up mainly of young men from New York, certainly caused a stir in Rimouski during those months in 1914 when they were based there. The salvage boats needed for operations were not used as lodging, but rather made almost daily round trips between Rimouski Harbour and the shipwreck site. While we don't know for certain where the men stayed during their time in Pointe-au-Père and Rimouski, it is most likely that they were in one or more of the smaller local hotels near the docks. The comfortable Château Tracy Hotel, across the street from the train station, was most probably used for the directors and chief engineers.

The initial shock of the sinking shook the little town of Rimouski, whose population had been talking of nothing else but the disaster since the early morning of 29 May. On the afternoon of Tuesday, 9 June, *Lady Evelyn* took a short cruise from Rimouski to the wreck site, allowing many citizens and a large part of the religious and civil elite to pay solemn tribute to the victims. Catholic and Protestant religious songs, speeches and prayers followed one another, and all descriptions of the moment speak of the immense emotion that gripped the crowd. It wasn't until mid-June that life returned to relative normalcy for the majority of the town's population.

The disaster had made the headlines all over the world, and newspapers and magazines in all languages reported on the tragedy on the St Lawrence. But nowhere else were the conversations dominated as much by the tragic fate of the British liner and her victims than in Canada, and especially Quebec. As one observer wrote on the back of a postcard dated 12 June, 'Québec City almost went crazy, but it's getting over it now'.[3]

Quebec City remained the centre of media attention for a time, as it was there that the Commission of Inquiry to better understand the circumstances of the accident opened at the Court House, a stone's throw from the Château Frontenac Hotel, on 16 June. The inquiry, presided over by Charles Bigham, Lord Mersey, was also expected to shed light on why the great liner sank so quickly, and to make recommendations to prevent such a tragedy from happening again.[4] This inquiry was instituted very quickly at the initiative of John Douglas

---

3 The postcard shows an image of *Empress of Ireland* on the front. Author's collection.
4 Lord Mersey would also preside over the inquiry into the sinking of RMS *Lusitania*, torpedoed by a German U-boat on 7 May 1915.

◄ *Lady Evelyn* leaving the harbour with dignitaries and students to visit the wreck site, 9 June 1914. (BANQ Rimouski, Fonds du Séminaire)

▼ Hymn-singing over the wreck, 9 June 1914. (BANQ Rimouski, Fonds du Séminaire)

Hazen, the Minister of Marine and Fisheries of Canada, under Part X of the Canada Shipping Act. The choice of Lord Mersey had been an obvious one, considering his previous mandate two years earlier, when he had chaired the British Commission of Inquiry into the sinking of *Titanic*. Justice Mersey had also been nominated as a member of the International Conference on Safety of Life at Sea (SOLAS) the previous year.[5] On 4 June, Hazen had already made arrangements to ask Lord Mersey to preside over the *Empress of Ireland* Commission of Inquiry – the Canadian Government wanted to move quickly to calm the growing rumours among the general

---

5   The resulting Convention on SOLAS was signed in January 1914.

Russian illustrated news magazine for 1 June 1914. (Author's collection)

public and in the media as to who was to blame for the accident, and also to reassure the world on the safety of the St Lawrence route.

Marie-Josephine, an 88ft-long, 125-ton schooner, was built at the Vital Charest shipyard in Rivière-du-Loup, Quebec, as a sailing schooner in 1891 under the name *T. Tremblay*. In 1913, she was refitted and converted into a steam schooner at the Fillion shipyard on the Island of Orleans for the shipowners Gagnon brothers of Saint-Paul Street in Quebec City. Renamed *Marie-Josephine*, after the Gagnon brothers' mother, she was officially registered as her property. The Gagnon brothers had long been active in diving in Quebec. In 1907, they had equipped several of the nineteen divers assigned to dive on the ruins of Quebec Bridge, following its tragic collapse. *Marie-Josephine* had also been used by the brothers Thomas and Edmond Tremblay, deep-sea divers from Quebec City, on some of their wreck-diving expeditions in the St Lawrence. The schooner was thus fully equipped for diving operations, and in the autumn of 1913, adverts had been published in Quebec City newspapers offering *Marie-Josephine* for sale or charter.[6]

This is how she ended up in Rimouski in June 1914, chartered by the Canadian Pacific Railway from the Gagnon brothers to serve as an operating base for the divers in following months. Her regular captain, Mr Arsenault, gave up his place for the duration of the operations over *Empress of Ireland* to Adam J. Davis, a twelve-year veteran of the US Navy and one of Wotherspoon's long-time main collaborators.

By 3 June, a complete police patrol of the south shore of the St Lawrence was established from the villages of Sainte-Luce to Sainte-Anne-des-Monts and, for weeks, debris and bodies of victims washed ashore and were

---

6   *Marie-Josephine* was still used for diving and salvage support when she burned and sank on the north shore of the St Lawrence in 1918.

recovered from the beaches. However, the majority of the victims' bodies were still trapped in the submerged hull of *Empress*, at the bottom of the St Lawrence. Among the missions entrusted to the Yankee Salvage Association by the Canadian Pacific Railway Company, the first was to recover the bodies of the victims, followed by the purser's safe and finally the 251 bars of silver contained in *Empress*' holds.

For some of the survivors of the sinking, it was time to resume the aborted voyage and the Canadian Pacific Railway arranged for their journey to the destination they wished to reach. For some, after this horrific ordeal, the only voyage they wanted to make was to get back home. Others still wanted to travel to Europe, and the company provided them with tickets on ships of the Allan Line and on the sister ship *Empress of Britain*. Survivor Walter Erzinger was booked on *Empress of Britain*, leaving Quebec on 11 June, in a stateroom close to the one he had on *Empress of Ireland* on the same deck. He could not sleep well that whole trip, and never came back to his life in Canada.

On 18 June 1914, sailors from HMS *Essex*, men from the Yankee Salvage Association and some local men began loading equipment on to *Marie-Josephine* and SS *Lord Strathcona* at the Pointe-au-Père Wharf in order to begin diving operations in earnest. The Yankee Salvage men, who had just arrived from New York and were settling in Rimouski for several weeks, had brought with them a number of trunks of personal items, which they had carried on to the wharf with the rest of the equipment.

▲ Lord Mersey (on the left) at Rideau Hall, Ottawa, as a guest of the Duchess of Connaught, June 1914. The duchess is standing in the middle, behind the chair. (Viscount Mersey, Bignor Park)

◄ The telegram received by Lord Mersey from J.D. Hazen, thanking him for consenting to preside over the inquiry into the sinking of *Empress of Ireland*. (Viscount Mersey, Bignor Park)

> *Marie-Josephine* in Rimouski Harbour. (Ralph S. Blydenburgh photo album, author's collection)

>> Survivors of *Empress of Ireland* posing together on the deck of *Empress of Britain* sailing to Europe, June 1914. From left to right: William Davies, Gordon Davidson, J.W. Swan, B. Byrne, James Johnson, Walter Erzinger. (Erzinger family, SHMP)

That same day, the large buoys that would be used for diving operations were transported to the Pointe-au-Père Wharf to be loaded on to *Marie-Josephine* and transported to the site of the disaster. The Pointe-au-Père lighthouse station, as well as the Port of Rimouski, would become the epicentre of the salvage operations during the summer and autumn of 1914. John McWilliams, acting as manager of the maritime station, agent for the shipping companies, telegraph operator and mayor of Pointe-au-Père, was involved in the work in various ways throughout the summer and autumn of 1914. He was one of the most prolific informers of the newspapers about the progress of the dives throughout the summer, using the wire telegraph station to send dispatches about the latest developments in the salvage operations.

The buoy installation operation was crucial to initiate the dives: in addition to marking the wreck site, they would be used to moor the boats during the work. Once loaded with buoys to be installed, *Marie-Josephine* left the Pointe-au-Père Wharf in the direction of the wreck site. Since 8 June, diving had been interrupted and each day that passed fed the impatience of the families who were waiting for the bodies of their loved ones to be recovered in order to finally mourn. Nevertheless, Wotherspoon did not want to give in to this pressure and it was crucial for him that the diving operations were well prepared.

In addition to the large buoys, diving pumps and other pieces of equipment, the decks of *Marie-Josephine* were occupied by large steam compressors manufactured by Ingersoll-Rand and the piping necessary for all operations requiring large quantities of compressed air. The schooner, already fitted for diving and salvage

Wilfred Whitehead (second from left), other sailors of HMS *Essex*, Captain Jean-Baptiste Bélanger of CGS *Eureka* (in the middle, back, with an officer cap), John Macdiarmid (second from left) and a few men from the Yankee Salvage Association, carrying a huge bundle of rope, which would be used to attach moorings to the wreck. (Ralph S. Blydenburgh photo album, author's collection)

Large buoys that will serve as mooring points are rolled on the Pointe-au-Père Wharf to be loaded on the salvage boats. In the background, from left to right, are the foghorn shed, the concrete lighthouse built in 1909 and the old lighthouse, built in 1867 and still fitted with its lantern on the roof. (Ralph S. Blydenburgh photo album, author's collection)

> *Marie-Josephine* leaving the wharf at Pointe-au-Père with the large mooring buoy cluttering a large part of her deck. (Ralph S. Blydenburgh photo album, author's collection)

▼ Taken on the same day as the previous photos, this view from another angle shows how, in addition to the buoys, technical equipment occupied almost the entire deck of *Marie-Josephine*. (Ralph S. Blydenburgh photo album, author's collection)

operations, was further loaded, notably by the addition of a decompression chamber.

Various ideas circulated in newspapers and technical magazines during those days about the future of the wreck and commentators speculated on the plans for it. One of the hypotheses considered was to partially raise *Empress* by inserting long canvas cushions under the hull that could be inflated with compressed air in order to make her slide. *Empress of Ireland* could then have been towed along the river bottom by powerful tugs on the surface and dragged back to shallower waters, which would have made it easier to recover the bodies and valuables. In shallower waters, one could even have tried to build watertight walls and empty the water around the wreck to work on her. This last option was

SS *Lord Strathcona* about to leave the Pointe-au-Père Wharf, loaded with diving equipment on 18 June 1914. (Ralph S. Blydenburgh photo album, author's collection)

the one used in 1912 on the wreck of USS *Maine* in Havana Harbour, a contract on which Wotherspoon had been hired as a consulting engineer. The first dives to *Empress* would serve to confirm the feasibility or not of these different options.

One of the powerful tugs that could have been used for this purpose was SS *Lord Strathcona*, owned by the Quebec Salvage and Wrecking Co., which was the official first responder when salvage services were needed on the St Lawrence. This Montreal-based company became the owner of the Davie shipbuilding and repair yard in Lauzon, Quebec, in 1912. George Duncan Davie, heir to the Davie operations, had remained superintendent of the company's marine salvage division until 1913, but from then on he concentrated on ship repair and construction. The command of the salvage, towing and refloating division was then passed to Haakon Kjerland, a Norwegian-born captain who already had extensive experience on the St Lawrence River. The Quebec Salvage and Wrecking Co. in purchasing all of Davie's assets, had taken over the contract that George Duncan Davie held from the government to assist ships in danger throughout the St Lawrence. The company's steamer *Lord Strathcona* would spend almost the entire navigation season deployed for this purpose.

The Davie salvage team first collaborated with King and Wotherspoon in 1907 during the salvage of the Allan Line's RMS *Bavarian*, but this time the work involved was of a very different nature, not least because of the high number of casualties that resulted from the disaster.

> The large mooring buoys marking the wreck site. (Ralph S. Blydenburgh photo album, author's collection)

▼ *Marie-Josephine* and *Lord Strathcona* moored over the wreck. (Fetherstonhaugh family)

The large buoys that were transported and installed on the dive site above the wreck of *Empress of Ireland* formed a rectangle that marked the area where the work was to be concentrated and would be left in place for the rest of the season. *Marie-Josephine* and *Lord Strathcona* also used these buoys to moor over the wreck during the dives. A whole flotilla of small boats, barges and rowboats was also kept on site for various tasks, including the recovery of floating debris.

On the first few days of diving, everyone found their bearings and there was good cooperation between the divers and workers of the Yankee Salvage Association and the naval divers of the HMS *Essex* team. Even if the tasks were rather gloomy and the circumstances difficult, the photographs taken during these first few days show a certain camaraderie between these men.

Among the first tasks to be accomplished on the site was inspecting the wreck as a whole in order to locate all the elements that could hinder the dives, install chains and moorings at certain strategic points and note as much information as possible about the exact position of the wreck on the bottom. During these first days, the divers took turns walking on the slanted hull and installing anchors for chains at the stern, the bow and near the navigation bridge. Without losing sight of the tasks to be accomplished in preparation for the operations that would last for weeks or even months, the divers were already bringing up some of the bodies that they spotted on the bottom as soon as they made their first descents.

During these first dives, on 19 June, HMS *Essex* diver Wilfred Whitehead brought up the first item salvaged from the wreck. While walking on the portside hull plates of *Empress*, Whitehead was instructed to walk from one end of his guideline to the other, while the crew on the surface would be able to follow his trail of air bubbles and thus determine with certainty the orientation of the wreck. Whitehead also looked for open portholes, as this was one of the questions that the inquiry into the sinking was interested to answer: were the portholes left open, thus accelerating the rate of water coming into the ship as she was sinking? As Whitehead did this, he noticed that almost all of the portholes he could find were closed, and one of them was even closed over a green silk curtain with a delicate birds and leaves design that seemed to be stuck halfway outside of the hull. He took his knife and cut that piece of curtain off, to bring it back to the surface. When he got back out of the water, he showed the piece of intricately embroidered cloth to everybody, and being the very first item salvaged, it created a great sensation among the people on the surface boats. Louis-Joseph Morault, a medical doctor from Rimouski who was there to assist the operations, was apparently very anxious to acquire the piece of curtain, but Whitehead emphatically told everyone that he intended to keep the little piece of cloth as a souvenir.[7]

Whitehead had also managed to bring up two bodies, which were handed over to Dr Morault. He made sure that they were summarily preserved with ice before being brought back to Rimouski Wharf by *Lord Strathcona*. The bodies were searched for clues to identify them. When it was not possible to identify them immediately, upon arrival in Rimouski each body was given a number, laid out on the dock facing the sun, described in detail and photographed. This documentation process could perhaps make it possible to identify them one day. The bodies were then entrusted to the care of local undertaker

The two team leaders, William Wallace Wotherspoon of the Yankee Salvage Association (seated centre left, with face in the sunlight) and John Macdiarmid of HMS *Essex* (the other face under the sunlight, on the right), preside over a festive table aboard *Marie-Josephine*, perhaps in honour of Wotherspoon, who had just celebrated his 40th birthday on 6 June 1914. The cook, standing behind Wotherspoon, is one of the key figures in the Yankee Salvage Association, having been part of most of the company's expeditions since 1908. (Ralph S. Blydenburgh photo album, author's collection)

---

7 Diver Whitehead told a reporter from his hometown, Huddersfield in Yorkshire, a year later, that he had turned down many tempting monetary offers for the souvenir. Not only did Whitehead keep the piece of cloth, but the precious relic is still in possession of his descendants, more than 110 years later. ('Distinction for Marsden Sailor', *Weekly Examiner*, Huddersfield, 13 March 1915, p.14).

The men of HMS *Essex*, in charge of their divers, work on the pumps and systems in front of the decompression chamber. On the right, wearing an officer's hat, is John Macdiarmid, HMS *Essex*'s dive team leader. (Ralph S. Blydenburgh photo album, author's collection)

Rimouski to the site of the wreck. Upon arrival on site, the rough sea, currents and winds prevented any attempt to dive safely. It was only around 2 p.m. that divers made their first dive. Two British divers from *Essex* and a diver from the Yankee Salvage Association team descended to the wreck. The Yankee salvage diver was Edward Edgar Cossaboom, 33, from Grand Manan, New Brunswick, Canada. He has been hired by the company a few weeks earlier. Cossaboom, a lifelong sailor, had been a fisherman, longshoreman and sailor, and had been diving for several years. Less than a month earlier, on 25 May, he crossed into the United States from Canada on SS *Ralph*, reaching New York to join Wotherspoon's team as a diver.[8] Little did he know that his first contract would bring him back to Canada – and would be his last.

Cossaboom was on his second dive of the day when, after half an hour on the bottom, his surface tenders tried to communicate with him by the usual means: sharp pulls on the rope he was supposed to be holding in his hand. Frederick Rogall, himself a diver, was his tender, in charge of monitoring his cables, and when Cossaboom did not respond, he alerted the British sailors to ask their divers to search for him. The divers of HMS *Essex*, much better equipped, had an underwater telephone and could communicate directly with the men on the surface. After another agonising half an hour, the two British divers came up empty-handed and exhausted. Cossaboom remained unaccounted for. The chief diver of HMS *Essex*, Wilfred Whitehead, then descended in turn with the sole mission of finding the unfortunate Canadian. He followed the same line that Cossaboom had used an hour earlier and retraced his steps once he reached the wreck.

Joseph Lepage, who proceeded with the embalming and who could see to the proper burial.

On 21 June, *Marie-Josephine* and *Lord Strathcona* were scheduled to cast off at 7 a.m. and steamed from

---

8   United States land border crossings registry for 1914. *Manifests of Alien Arrivals at Eastport, Fort Kent, Lubec, and Madawaska, Maine, ca. 1906–December 1952*. NARA microfilm publication A3401, 2 rolls. NAID: 4492740. Records of the Immigration and Naturalization Service, RG 85; The National Archives in Washington, DC.

With the British divers underwater, an officer is communicating with them using the submarine telephone. The tug *Lord Strathcona* is in the background. (Ralph S. Blydenburgh photo album, author's collection)

Unsure of his whereabouts, in complete darkness and now at the bottom of the river about 140ft below, Whitehead finally found Cossaboom, unconscious. He tied a rope around his waist and brought him to the surface.[9] Whitehead, in a bid to rush to the surface, did not take the time to do any decompression and apparently suffered a severe case of barodontalgia, commonly known among divers as a 'tooth squeeze'.[10] On *Marie-Josephine*, Dr Louis-Joseph Morault tried everything he could to revive the unfortunate Cossaboom. The decompression chamber was even used, but it was clear that *Empress of Ireland* had just claimed another life. Cossaboom, in only a few days of diving, had managed to go over most of the wreck, to attach an anchor chain to the stern of *Empress* and to bring up a few bodies of victims. He had also determined that *Empress* was lying in about 14ft of mud and confirmed that her bow was pointing north-east.

The unfortunate diver most likely lost his footing on the slippery hull of *Empress* and fell to the bottom. As he fell, he went from a depth of 80ft to 140ft in one fell swoop. Knowing that the sudden change in air pressure in his diving suit could be fatal, he likely tried to open the air control valve on his helmet, turned it the wrong way and cut himself off from the surface air supply. The poor man, in a panic, forced the valve until it broke off.

---

9 Wilfred Whitehead was congratulated by Lord Mersey at the inquiry for this act of courage. He would also later receive a King's Silver Medal for bravery at sea for his attempt to rescue Cossaboom.

10 Whitehead, a year later, gave an interview to a reporter in his hometown and said that he had lost some teeth as a result of the event. ('A Worthy Seaman', *Weekly Examiner*, Huddersfield, Saturday, 17 April 1915, p.15).

This is believed to be the only photo of Cossaboom (on the left), taken on *Marie-Josephine*, June 1914. (Pat Whitehead)

As soon as Cossaboom died, the decision was made to re-evaluate the continuation of the salvage work. The testimony of Wotherspoon, Whitehead and John Macdiarmid, chief diver of HMS *Essex*, to the Commission of Inquiry into the sinking of *Empress* in Quebec City provided the pretext to bring everyone back to shore and take a step back to consider what to do next. The divers of the expedition and the other members of the team were shaken by what had happened to their comrade. A pause would be salutary for the whole team. On 22 June, while Cossaboom's body was being returned to his family to be taken back to Grand Manan to be buried, Wotherspoon, Macdiarmid and Whitehead headed to Quebec City by train, while the Yankee Salvage team followed them a few hours later on board *Lord Strathcona*.

Wotherspoon testified before the Commission of Inquiry in the criminal courtroom of the Quebec City Courthouse on the morning of 23 June. Dressed entirely in black as a tribute to Cossaboom, Wotherspoon explained the efforts made by the New Brunswick diver to place the buoys necessary for the dives and to perfectly locate and describe the position of the wreck on the bottom. Lawyer Charles Haight, also a New Yorker, who was defending the owners of *Storstad*, asked him many questions about the exact location of the wreck and the possibility that *Empress* could have changed position or drifted while sinking. Wotherspoon then explained how *Empress* lay on the bottom and that, according to him, the currents could have had a great influence on the position of the ship between the surface and the bottom of the river.

Haight had tried to demonstrate that *Empress* had cut across *Storstad*'s path and was lying on the bottom of the river in the north-eastern direction, which corresponded to the *Storstad* crew's version of the accident. During his testimony, Wotherspoon confirmed instead that the currents were strong at this location and that, in his opinion, under the tidal conditions at the time of the sinking on the night of 29 May, *Empress* could have turned her stern toward the shore while sinking. In any case, the wreck could not provide much more information to explain the circumstances of the accident. Wotherspoon also used his testimony to confirm that *Empress* could not be refloated and that the damage caused by the collision was impossible to inspect because the wreck was lying on her starboard side – the side of that fatal breach. Macdiarmid then testified and essentially corroborated Wotherspoon's testimony regarding the position of the

AUGUSTUS McGUIRE

For Wotherspoon, Cossabom's death must surely have brought back to mind the death of another diver employed by the company only a few months earlier. Augustus McGuire, a diver born in Maine in 1856, was an employee of the Yankee Salvage Association on the ship SS *Forward*. In September 1913, *Forward* was at sea off North Carolina when a leak was spotted in the ship's hull. McGuire descended under the hull in an attempt to seal the breach, but was unsuccessful at first. After surfacing, and against the advice of Wotherspoon, who found him nervous and tired, McGuire decided to attempt a second dive. After some time underwater, the men who were supplying him with air and monitoring his lifeline noticed that he did not seem to be moving. They decided to hoist him to the surface. Despite attempts by Wotherspoon and the other crew members to revive him, everyone realised that McGuire was dead. Unable to embalm him and unable to resign himself to burying him at sea in the event that the family claimed the body, Wotherspoon contacted the nearest lighthouse station by wireless telegraph. The keeper of the Ocracoke lighthouse answered and began preparations to land the victim on the nearby island. There, a doctor could only certify the death and preside over the burial of the diver in the tiny local cemetery.[1] A few months later, the incident made headlines in Perth Amboy, New Jersey, McGuire's hometown. The diver's widow publicly accused the Yankee Salvage Association of negligence and claimed that the burial on Ocracoke Island had only served to hide the true circumstances of her husband's death. The case quickly disappeared from the local news after the release of a letter from the Ocracoke doctor, who defended the company and suggested that the heart problem that killed him had occurred quite naturally. Nevertheless, McGuire's and now Cossaboom's death must have destabilised Wotherspoon and cast a serious shadow on the whole operation in Rimouski.

SS *Forward*, Yankee Salvage Association's salvage schooner. (Ralph S. Blydenburgh photo album, author's collection)

---

1 This story has become a legend on Ocracoke Island, where the 'old diver' is said to haunt the island and its cemetery. A diving boot that belonged to McGuire is on display at the local museum and, for over 100 years, children on the island have been scaring each other by hiding near the cemetery and shouting 'Old Diver, Old Diver, what do you say?' According to legend, every now and then a man's voice answers, 'Nothing'! (The Ocracoke Preservation Society website, accessed 2 October 2022, www.ocracokepreservationsociety.org.)

The Commission of Inquiry presided over by John Charles Bigham, Lord Mersey. (Viscount Mersey, Bignor Park)

wreck. He added, however, that based on the observations of his divers, most of the portholes on *Empress* were closed and therefore could not have contributed significantly to sinking the ship so quickly.

Diver Wilfred Whitehead took the stand next, telling of his missions during his dive, and of the recovery of Cossaboom's body. Lord Mersey showed a particular interest in the piece of green silk brought up by Whitehead, asking him if the fact that the curtain was sticking out meant that the porthole was opened or closed. Whitehead explained to the Commission that the curtain was stuck outside the hull, with the porthole closed over it from inside. Most, if not all, portholes appeared to Whitehead to have been closed.

HMS *Essex* had diverted her mission to assist the Canadian authorities following the *Empress* disaster, and remained anchored off Quebec City, while only her team of divers were in Rimouski. Cossaboom's death prompted the Royal Navy officers to reflect on their further involvement in the operations. Captain Hugh

D.R. Watson sent his lieutenant to Rimouski to see the situation for himself and to discuss with Canadian Pacific officials. His report back to Captain Watson was clear: the operation was risky and nothing more could be done to salvage the wreckage or raise the bodies of the victims by the *Essex* sailors. Captain Watson therefore announced that the British divers would have to stop work in Rimouski and return on board before the end of June, confirming that they would not exceed the two-week involvement that they had initially promised. The Yankee Salvage Association would be the only one to continue the operations from that moment on.

For Wotherspoon, the news of the imminent departure of *Essex*'s divers required a review of his own team's involvement. Not only were the *Essex* divers among the best in the world, but they had the best equipment, especially thanks to their team leader, Macdiarmid. Wotherspoon reminded the Commission of Inquiry that Macdiarmid was one of the professors involved in decompression and deep-sea-diving research: 'Not only

▲ This is the only known photo showing HMS *Essex* at anchor in Quebec City, June 1914. (*Canadian Courier*, 13 June 1914)

◂ Wilfred Whitehead (standing), c.1914. (Pat Whitehead)

has he the gear that one would naturally expect the vessel to have but, on account of his experience, I take it that he rather took a little more care in selecting it so that it is quite the best.'[11] Wotherspoon himself ordered, directly from Great Britain, equipment equivalent to that used by the British, probably under the advice of Macdiarmid. The difficulty of diving in the particular conditions of the river required the latest technology, rigorous preparation and a larger number of trusted divers.

The meeting between North American and British Navy divers above *Empress* created a remarkable exchange of practices and technology. The occasion of this unlikely meeting was unique. While the North Americans admired some of Britain's technological equipment, British divers dived the cold waters of the St Lawrence with their bare hands. It was the Americans from the Yankee Salvage Association who suggested that they wear rubber gloves, which now seems commonplace and trivial, but was quite an innovation at the time. What's more, the British still only used manual air pumps to supply air to their divers, while the Americans increasingly relied on mechanical compressors for this task. One thing is for sure: the skill, courage and resourcefulness of the British sailors had been much appreciated by the Americans, who dubbed them the 'Handy Men'. But now, the planned departure of these 'Handy Men' radically altered the plans of the Yankee Salvage Association.

---

11   Testimony of William Wallace Wotherspoon at the Commission of Inquiry, question 6363.

Wilfred Whitehead, on the left, is helping Keller prepare to descend on the wreck, bare-handed. (Ralph S. Blydenburgh photo album, author's collection)

July

On 30 June, after a few final dives that brought up more bodies, the sailors of *Essex* returned to their ship anchored in the Port of Quebec. Wotherspoon had to prepare the next steps himself. He instructed his divers to prioritise the recovery of bodies when they were reachable, but not to go too far into the wreck because of the risks involved. For the items in the salvage contract – the safe, the 251 bars of silver and the mailbags – a hole would have to be drilled in the side of the hull to reach the specie room and the mailroom, located in the same section of the ship.

On 2 July, the new diving gear ordered from Great Britain arrived in Rimouski. The team had access to plans of the ship, but this was not enough. The wreck was lying on her starboard side and the divers had to move around in the darkness of the river bottom. To enhance their safety and ensure the success of the recovery mission, Wotherspoon's team had to find ways to become more familiar with the ship's interior configuration. On the night of 2–3 July, *Empress of Ireland*'s sister ship, *Empress of Britain*, sailed up the river toward Quebec City and stopped off at Rimouski for about thirty minutes. Wotherspoon and a few men from his team boarded the ship to visit and explore her interior, in order to familiarise themselves with her deck layout and clearly identify the passage that would lead them to the specie room. Guided by officers of *Empress of Britain*, the men took notes and integrated as much information as possible to give them a sense of the interior spaces of the lost ship as they visited her identical twin. *Empress of Britain* also carried the new diving equipment ordered from Great Britain by Wotherspoon, and the wooden crates containing these precious devices were unloaded on to *Lady Evelyn* and brought to Rimouski Pier at the same time.

JOSEPH McGOLDRICK

While the summer of 1914 photographs included in the Yankee Salvage Association album most likely were taken by multiple photographers, mostly from Rimouski, some were reputedly taken by Joseph McGoldrick, son of a New Jersey captain and himself a sailor. A rowdy character, McGoldrick, at the age of 27 in August 1910, had been intoxicated in a local bar in the heart of the Irish community of Perth Amboy, New Jersey. He was arrested for public disorder after he threatened a bartender with a gun when he had been refused another drink, and later threatened the policeman who was called to restrain him. It took the intervention of McGoldrick's influential father to get him off the charges. However, this episode seems to have allowed young Joseph to get his act together and he got married the following year. He was then hired by the Yankee Salvage Association as an able seaman. When he arrived in Rimouski, Joseph had just lost his older sister, who died in April 1914 of a long illness.

On 12 April 1915, he presented the picture seen here to a contest organised by the *New York Herald* newspaper, specifying that he had taken it himself. Although it is hard to confirm if he was, indeed, behind the lens for that or any other photo, McGoldrick nonetheless received a prize of $3 for this submission.[1] He would later die in February 1918 when the US Navy tug on which he served was lost at sea. Two other McGoldrick brothers died in the First World War.

The photo of a Royal Navy diver and his tenders submitted to a photographic contest in 1915. (Ralph S. Blydenburgh photo album, author's collection)

---

1   'McGoldrick Tries for Prize in Photographic Contest', *Perth Amboy Evening News*, Perth Amboy, New Jersey, 13 April 1915, p.4. The photo itself was republished by some other papers in the following days, including: 'Divers Salvaging for Cargo of the Wrecked *Empress of Ireland*', *Harrisburg Star-Independent*, Harrisburg, Pennsylvania, 13 April 1915, p.12.

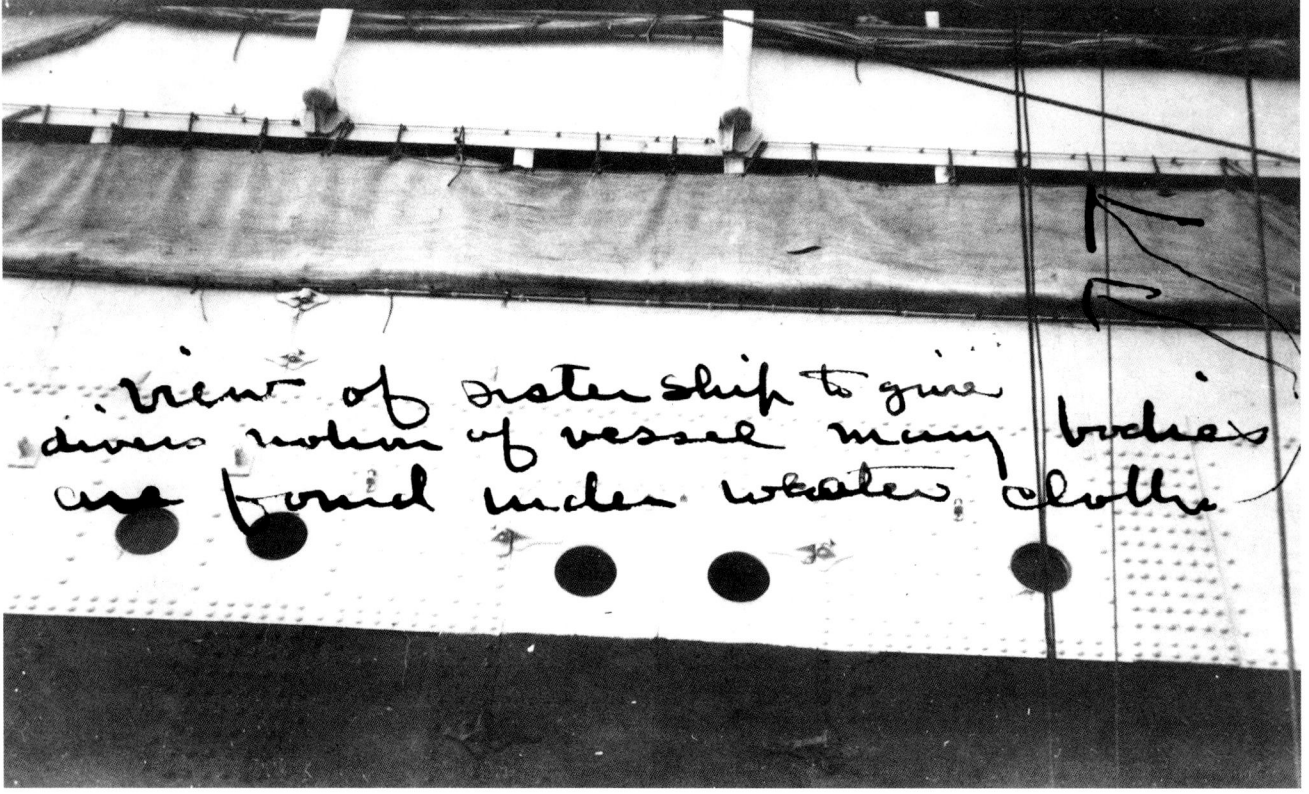

Photo of *Empress of Britain* on the morning of 3 July, hand-annotated by William W. Wotherspoon, who wrote: 'View of sister ship to give divers notion of vessel. Many bodies are found under weather clothe [*sic*]'. (Canadian Museum of History, 2012-H0018.301)

It was there, on Rimouski Wharf, on the morning of 3 July 1914, that a large quantity of new material received from the Siebe-Gorman Company in Great Britain was set and displayed for a photographer. Siebe-Gorman was one of the main manufacturers of underwater diving equipment in the world. In addition to the two diving suits, an underwater electric telephone system was included, which would make it possible to rely on this technology still, now that the sailors of HMS *Essex* had left a few days before with their own telephone. Some North American divers had remarked that they wouldn't want to bother with an extra cable to the surface and weren't keen on the idea of using the phone. But the accident that claimed Cossaboom's life a few days earlier proved to the whole team beyond doubt the need for such a communication system between divers and the surface. The small box contained batteries and a system of electric bells and switches that not only rang the diver on the bottom from the surface, but also enabled two divers on the bottom to communicate with each other at the same time, with the help of the operator on the surface.

While it is true that several cables and hoses connected the divers to the surface, by far the most important was, of course, the air-supply hose. A combination of manual and mechanical pumps were used throughout the operation. Most divers preferred manual pumps, which were more adaptable to specific situations and pressure requirements. Mechanical pumps were, at first, used mainly to operate all the air-pressure machinery and underwater tools used in deep-sea operations.

Brand-new diving equipment, fresh out of the crates, is photographed for posterity on Rimouski Pier, 3 July 1914. (Ralph S. Blydenburgh photo album, author's collection)

The new submarine telephone from Siebe-Gorman was especially important for the safety of divers. (Ralph S. Blydenburgh photo album, author's collection)

Testing and inspecting one of the mechanical pumps on *Marie-Josephine*. Ralph S. Blydenburgh, smoking a pipe, is supervising the tests. (Ralph S. Blydenburgh photo album, author's collection)

The hand pump allowed air pressure to be adjusted as required and did not depend on complex mechanical operation.

Although *Marie-Josephine* was equipped for diving operations as early as 1913, she had to be supplied with even more specialised equipment by Canadian Pacific for an endeavour as complex as the one in the summer of 1914. The owners of *Empress of Ireland* also received invoices from the Yankee Salvage Association for some of the equipment that they needed. In turn, Canadian Pacific added these amounts to the claims made against the owners of *Storstad*. State-of-the-art technology and techniques were at the heart of the operation, and nothing was spared to ensure the safety of divers.

From the first week of July, the work became more systematic and organised. The Yankee Salvage Association's team of divers was increased to seven, all from the United States and Canada, including one from Quebec: Edmond Tremblay. They worked in rotation, giving priority to bringing up the bodies of the victims, and then beginning the preparation, at the bottom of the river, for the complex mission of penetrating the wreck to salvage the valuables.

During all operations, small boats were on site and used to collect what the divers brought to the surface and to assist them while they worked below, especially when they moved a good distance on the bottom. What these boats had to carry was macabre, as the corpses found by the divers were numerous, all through those first few weeks of July especially. Even a lifeboat from *Empress of Ireland* was used over the wreck to recover the bodies brought up by the divers.

UNDERWATER TECHNOLOGY

Underwater exploration has always been a human pursuit, particularly for recovering sunken goods and salvaging wrecks. As soon as hand pumps capable of compressing air sufficiently to withstand the pressure of the depths became available in the late eighteenth century, inventors began experimenting with models for deep-sea divers. One of these pioneers was Augustus Siebe, a German-born but naturalised British engineer, who perfected the diving suit to the point of developing a two-section helmet in 1837. This became the standard on which subsequent developments were based. By the end of the nineteenth century, Siebe-Gorman, the company he founded with his son-in-law William Augustus Gorman, was the world's leading manufacturer and distributor of diving equipment.

In Canada, Montreal tinsmith John Date developed his own diving suits, in particular to meet the needs of divers working on the construction of the Victoria Bridge between 1854 and 1857. His equipment quickly gained an excellent reputation, and by the time of his death in 1909, John Date Industries was recognised as one of the leading manufacturers and providers of diving equipment in North America.

In 1914, this technology from the first half of the nineteenth century was still the norm, even though materials, equipment and construction had been greatly improved and standardised. For all intents and purposes, it wasn't until the democratisation of scuba diving in the mid-twentieth century that the technology of hardhat diving was superseded.

The basic equipment of the hardhat diver consisted of a brass helmet in two sections, the bonnet and breastplate. This bonnet, pierced by portholes, also included valves and pressurised air-line connectors. At the beginning of the twentieth century, these helmets weighed an average of 40lb. The weight of the helmet served to compensate for the large volume of internal air, and thus made the helmet neutrally buoyant. The weight was a necessity. Contemporary helmets are made of fibreglass, but

John Date, right, demonstrating his equipment at the 1876 Philadelphia World's Fair. (Mike Babiski)

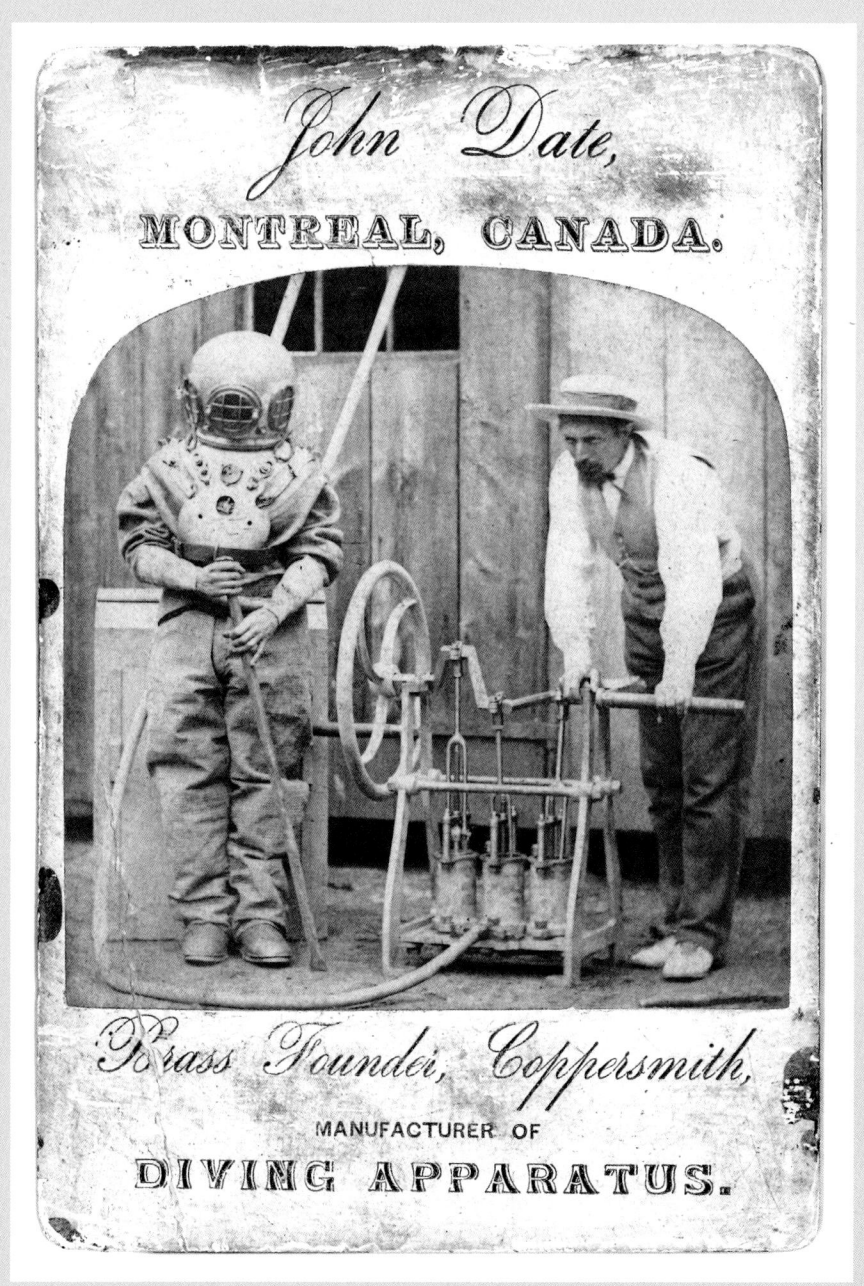

with added weight, for the same reason as before. In addition to this enormous weight, the diver also wore leather shoes with heavy metal soles (lead or brass). A pair of these shoes could weigh up to 40lb. Other weights, often worn on a belt or harness, helped the diver to walk on the river bed without floating. Such weight, enormous on the surface, was felt much more lightly by the diver once in the water. A suit, made of rubber-lined canvas, waterproof and relatively flexible, completed the outfit.

In North America, pressure is generally measured in psi, and the convention is to calculate water pressure using the pressure exerted by a 10m water column as a basis, i.e. 14.7 psi. This measurement is equivalent to one atmosphere. As the diver descends underwater, the ambient pressure increases at the rate of 14.7 psi for every 10m. In salt water, a diver descending to a depth of around 130ft, as on *Empress of Ireland*, will feel a pressure equivalent to 5 atmospheres, or 60lb per square inch. The pressurised air supply, provided by a pump on the surface, enables them to breathe easily, but also to combat this water pressure by maintaining an equivalent pressure inside their suit and helmet. The entry and exit of compressed air into the suit is controlled by the diver directly via valves on the helmet. This pressure balance is crucial at all times, and communication between the diver and the surface is vital.[1]

---

1   For an excellent reference to the basics of deep-sea diving, contemporary to the *Empress of Ireland* salvage operations: G.D. Stillson, *Report on Deep Diving Tests*, US Government Printing Office, Washington DC, 1915.

The deck of *Marie-Josephine* photographed from her main mast. Among the clutter visible, one will note some Ingersoll-Rand compressors, the decompression chamber and some of the divers' suits that can be seen drying. (Ralph S. Blydenburgh photo album, author's collection)

Small craft rowing over the wreck waiting for the divers to come back up. (Fetherstonhaugh family)

Three makeshift coffins are laid across the edge of this *Empress of Ireland* lifeboat alongside *Marie-Josephine*, ready to receive human remains. (Mariners' Museum)

The body of a victim lifted on to a rowboat. (Ralph S. Blydenburgh photo album, author's collection)

The bodies were lifted on to rowboats before being placed on *Lord Strathcona* to be transported to Rimouski. A makeshift stretcher, made of heavy timber, planks and canvas tarpaulins, was used to hoist the bodies aboard the boats. The weight allowed the stretcher to be sunk into the river so divers could place the body on to them. Tarpaulins made it possible to hold together and hide the bodies which, after weeks at the bottom of the river at the mercy of marine animals, especially snow crabs, were terribly decomposed and often unrecognisable. This dismal task was repeated around 118 times during the summer of 1914.[12]

In Rimouski and Pointe-au-Père, even though the shipwreck had taken place more than a month before, *Empress of Ireland* was still in the daily life of the inhabitants. The comings and goings of trains and boats continued to fuel conversations and brought visitors to the small town. A lot of people came into town from all over North America in the hope that the body of a relative or a friend would be brought to the surface by divers. During the first week of July, some of them were even brought on board *Marie-Josephine* and given direct access to Wotherspoon and some of his team in order to provide more details on the people they were looking for. A brother of prominent Montreal first-class passenger Henry Herbert Lyman pointed to deck plans of the *Empress* staterooms 4 and 6 occupied by Lyman and his wife and described pieces of jewellery the two might have worn that night.[13] Wotherspoon patiently met with these grieving strangers, noted and kept the information they left with him, but had to explain to them, respectfully,

---

12 This figure comes from a note, written in 1914 on the back of a photo in the collection of the Rimouski Catholic Seminary, where the observer (most probably Joseph Lepage, the Rimouski undertaker) notes: '... bodies recovered "118", among which 93 buried in the C.P.R. cemetery at Pointe-au-Père, 7 Catholic buried in this town's cemetery, 8 sent over'. The figures do not add up to 118, but rather to 108. The number of bodies buried in Pointe-au-Père and Rimouski (93 and 7) are verified, but since it is impossible to verify the number of bodies claimed as sent over to families, for lack of record and archival sources, we cannot be sure if the typo is '108' instead of '118' or '8' instead of '18'. So the number 118 used in the book is to be considered as an estimate. (Archives Nationales du Québec, Rimouski, Fonds du Séminaire.)

13 'Divers Will Be Shown all Over *Empress* Liner', *The Montreal Star*, 2 July 1914, p.7.

WHOSE ALBUM WAS IT?

Dont look at this one

The small piece of paper over a macabre image. The photo it warned against is reproduced overleaf. (Ralph S. Blydenburgh photo album, author's collection)

When the photo album was acquired, there was no way of knowing to whom it had belonged. Of course, the link with the Yankee Salvage Association was easy to make, but the album, partly dismantled, had been taken out of context on the auction site. Furthermore, the seller had bought it herself from another person who had no information about it, and above all, absolutely nothing was written anywhere in the album. The photos were not identified, there were no handwritten annotations, no dates: nothing. One particular man appeared in many photographs in the album, but it was impossible to know who that was. Could this man posing with the silver ingots salvaged from *Empress*, dressed as a gentleman, be the one who put the album together? Was it Wotherspoon himself? Was it Robert Gregg Skerrett, the journalist who wrote a lot of articles about *Empress of Ireland* salvage operations? At the beginning of this research, no good-quality photos of any of these men were known.

Only one written exception appeared in the album and would eventually be the key to solve the mystery. To hide the macabre photo of a body pulled up from *Empress of Ireland*, the owner of the album had pasted an opaque flap of paper on which he had written, by hand: 'Dont look at this one.' One photo pulled out of the album and sold before the album was purchased, fortunately scanned by the seller, revealed another piece of handwriting on the back. The photo showed USS *Yankee* and had been used as a postcard, written in the same handwriting as the little opaque piece of paper, and was signed 'Ralph' and addressed to a Mrs E.R. Blydenburgh. Ralph had written to his mother while working on *Yankee*! After a few more days of research, I followed a few leads to a Ralph Blydenburgh, including a record of his position as secretary on the board of the Yankee Salvage Association. The confirmation came when I stumbled upon a photo of a wedding reception in 1946, which Ralph Stratton Blydenburgh had attended. There was the man in the album, of course older and with a bit more weight, but he still had the exact same facial features and smile as on the famous photo with the silver ingots taken in Rimouski in 1914. The man who appeared in several photos and who had soberly covered a photo that was difficult for the faint of heart to look at was Ralph Stratton Blydenburgh. The research had just taken a decisive turn.

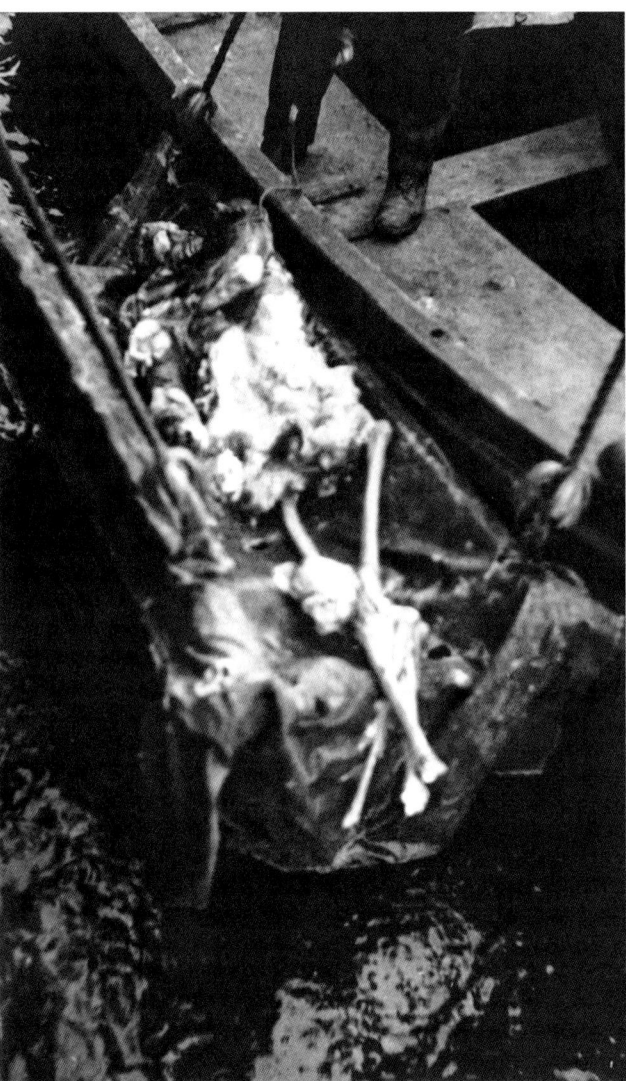

A body is lifted out of the water to be put on a small craft. This is the photo that was hidden in the album. (Ralph S. Blydenburgh photo album, author's collection)

that the chances of recovering bodies were extremely slim if the victims had not left their cabins during the sinking. Under no circumstance would the divers be allowed to venture into the maze of corridors and passages inside the wreck, and only the easily accessible gangways and companionways would be searched. Even the simple act of opening a door was a tremendous task at these depths, a task that would use the whole time of one dive for a man to accomplish. As the *Montreal Star* writer penned it: 'Those who are still in the cabins are resting in the only graves they will ever find.'[14]

On 7 July, on a letterhead of the Château Tracy Hotel, located just across the street from Rimouski train station, Richard Fisher wrote to his sister and brother-in-law in Great Britain. Fisher had left Chicago for Rimouski to assist in the recovery of the bodies in the hope that those of his mother, Margaret, and his brother, Wilfred, who were both travelling separately on *Empress* (the mother in second class, the son in third), would be brought up by divers.

He wrote:

The divers have got 15 bodies so far and the tug boat as a rule comes into port between 3 to 5 in the afternoons and yesterday they only got 1 lady and you could not identify her by her face the fish had almost eaten her away only her overcoat looked good but only the makers' name could be found on it. Yesterday afternoon, I helped to bury 2 bodies one was an old man about 60 and the other a young woman about 25. There was only 4 of us that could speak English the rest was all French. The American Consul read the services. The CPR [Canadian Pacific Railway] have bought the piece

---

14 'Divers Will Be Shown all Over *Empress* Liner', *The Montreal Star*, July 1914, p.7.

Lord Strathcona, moored to the 'wreck' buoy, is standing by in case bodies are brought to the surface by divers. (Fetherstonhaugh family)

of land almost opposite where the *Empress* went to her finish. The bodies that they bury here in Father Point is all numbered, photographed and a full description and any rings or anything like that is kept by themselves and numbered same as the coffin as no doubt half of them that they bury will be claimed and taken away again.[15] […] There is two fellows here from Alberta looking for their wives there too, Swedish people. […] When I stand on the end of the Pier I can see the divers working, although it's quite a distance, but only 4 miles from Father Point. It takes me an hour to walk to Father Point from my hotel.[16]

Lord Strathcona was mobilised for forty-six full days over the wreck, between 30 May and 30 August 1914. It was this boat that returned to the Port of Rimouski each afternoon to bring back the recovered bodies, while *Marie-Josephine* could remain above the wreck sometimes overnight, when conditions were good.

---

15   This, unfortunately, never happened. The sixty-eight unidentified bodies in Pointe-au-Père, the three others in Rimouski and the thirty-nine more in Quebec City are still there, and not one case of exhumation after identification has been recorded.
16   This letter is archived with the Fisher family papers, and quoted with permission from Gareth Abel Bunting.

Château Tracy Hotel in Rimouski, across the street from the train station. (Author's collection)

Since Rimouski did not have a Protestant officiant, one was brought in from Fraserville (now Rivière-du-Loup), a town 100km west, to consecrate the lot acquired by Canadian Pacific on the shore of the river, and to proceed with the burials in this dedicated cemetery. The lot had been purchased from a local farmer, but until 1893 was part of an estate owned by Lord Mount Stephen, a former builder and director of the Canadian Pacific Railway. When it was possible to identify the recovered victims as being Catholic, either by formal identification or simply by a religious sign found on the remains, they were entrusted to the care of the parish priest of Saint-Germain de Rimouski. Canadian Pacific, later that summer, purchased another lot for the Catholic victims at the parish cemetery, in the centre of Rimouski.[17]

The Salvation Army, hard hit by the disaster, remained represented in Rimouski for several weeks in order to do its utmost to bring back the remains to the affected families. For this purpose, two officers of the Canadian Salvation Army, Major Townshend and Major Jennings, spent part of their summer on the *Marie-Josephine* and

---

17   This cemetery was located not too far from the train station in 1914, but with the expansion of the town, was later relocated further east, where it is remains today. The *Empress of Ireland* Catholic victims, memorial stone and bodies were moved to that new parish cemetery in 1951.

SS *Lord Strathcona* is moored alongside *Marie-Josephine* at Rimouski Pier. (Ralph S. Blydenburgh photo album, author's collection)

Lord Strathcona salvage boats waiting to see if the divers would bring up bodies of Salvationists.

After the underwriters gave their permission to drill into the hull, on 10 July preparation of the area where a hole would be made in *Empress*' side plating began in earnest. The first step was to locate the porthole leading to the cross-corridor that would be used to remove the valuables. To do this, the divers walked the hull from bow to stern using markers and counting the number of portholes. Once the right spot was located, it was marked with guide lines. These operations alone required a large number of dives and the work was tedious.

A wooden platform was then installed on the angled hull plates to work flat along the port side of the hull to drill, one hole at a time, into the ¾in-thick steel wall. A powerful hydraulic drill, nicknamed 'Little David', was used to open the steel plates of the hull from the side. The holes, close to one another, were made with the drill, and then a saw was used to finish detaching completely a 6ft × 12ft section of steel plate from the hull. Steel eyelets

▲ Two divers from Yankee Salvage getting ready to go down to the wreck (the one on the right is William Lutz). On the right, just behind the man with the binoculars, are two officers of the Salvation Army. (Ralph S. Blydenburgh photo album, author's collection)

▶ A 'Little David' drill on the deck of *Marie-Josephine*. (Ralph S. Blydenburgh photo album, author's collection)

were then attached to the corners of the freed plate so that it could be pulled up to the surface with winches and the hull was thus opened like a tin can. Although the use of explosives was considered at times during the preparations, they were not used in the end, contrary to what many may have believed for a long time.[18] In fact, the use of explosives would have been the last resort, but it was deemed too difficult to control, as it would have made damage to the hull and interior passages very random and could have left sharp and dangerous sections of sheet metal. Furthermore, Canadian Pacific wished to avoid – if possible – the massive use of dynamite, given the presence of the victims' bodies. It is nevertheless possible, but difficult to prove, that small quantities of explosives may have been used, in particular to force open certain loading doors along the hull, in order to facilitate the recovery of bodies. In the complete list of claims for costs and reimbursements related to the sinking and submitted to the courts by the Canadian Pacific Railway, we find a claim for $8.73 worth of dynamite, submitted by the Talbot Company Limited. Even at the time, this amount was minimal, so whatever purpose was served

---

18   Most books on *Empress of Ireland* picked up this explosive story, most probably from Wotherspoon himself who, in 1939, mentioned the use of explosives in his recollection of the events of the summer of 1914 for the book *Men Under the Sea*, by Admiral Edward Ellsberg. Prior to 1939, dynamite was almost never mentioned in serious sources, except to state that it would not be used given the risks.

Rimouski undertaker and photographer Joseph Lepage poses in his own studio with two Canadian Pacific police officers, Sergeants MacFarland and Irvine. (BANQ Rimouski, Fonds du Séminaire de Rimouski [P60])

by this dynamite, the quantity of explosives involved was negligible and not sufficient to blast open the side of the wreck.[19]

To complete his team's equipment, Wotherspoon only lacked electric underwater lamps, which were seen as absolutely essential in the difficult diving conditions. Indeed, the average visibility at this depth and in this part of the St Lawrence River is only around 10ft. Wotherspoon made the round trip to New York himself to bring back these electric torches and returned with two new divers, who completed the team on 14 July. The investment necessary to obtain and mobilise all this advanced technology was tremendous. The large number of photos that depict this hi-tech, brand-new equipment show how proud Wotherspoon was of it and how critical the role of technology was in safely and efficiently conducting these operations.

The most impressive piece of equipment available to the Yankee Salvage Association during these operations was certainly the decompression chamber. In his

19   LAC-BAC, Court of the Exchequer, 59M.

▲ A Yankee Salvage Association deckhand testing an underwater lamp. (Ralph S. Blydenburgh photo album, author's collection)

▶ A close-up view of one of the underwater electric torch lights. (Ralph S. Blydenburgh photo album, author's collection)

name on ship-refloating techniques. The decompression chamber allowed divers to return to the surface for mandatory decompression, instead of having to do it in decompression stops underwater. After their average thirty–forty-minute dives, at depths of around 80–120ft, divers returned to the surface on *Marie-Josephine* and were then helped to remove some of their equipment and enter the decompression chamber as quickly as possible. In this chamber, their bodies were brought back to the pressure of the riverbed, then gradually decompressed.

Wotherspoon made other changes to the conduct of operations after the accident that took the life of diver Cossaboom. From that moment on, divers began descending in pairs instead of doing solo dives. This tandem work allowed at least one of the two divers to immediately report a problem or to come to the aid of a comrade in case of need. Throughout the summer, the difficulties of the mission and the conditions of the St Lawrence forced Wotherspoon and his men to adopt and adapt new techniques and technologies as the work progressed and problems arose.

The biggest challenge facing the divers, therefore, was access to the rooms where the purser's safe, bullion and mailbags were stowed, right in the heart of the ship. The safe would be a particular challenge, as it was installed in a special niche in a secure room designed to make it difficult for anyone to access, even in normal conditions, with the ship floating upright. At the bottom of the river, in a wreck leaning on her starboard side, in the dark and with deep-sea-diving suits connected to the surface, one can easily imagine the difficulty of the task. In addition to visiting the sister ship, *Empress of Britain*, to familiarise themselves with the interior of the wreck, Wotherspoon and his men planned their entry by studying the ship's

unpublished autobiography, Robert Owen King states that this was the first time in the world that such a chamber had been used on a boat in a salvage operation at sea.[20] William Ebeling was responsible for inspecting all the equipment and pumps on a daily basis and ensuring their proper operation.[21] He was one of the main architects of the technical successes of the Yankee Salvage Association and even had a few patents to his

---

20 Autobiography of R.O. King, cited here with the permission of Professor Galen Perras, PhD, who allowed me to consult the manuscript.
21 Born in Germany, William Ebeling immigrated to the United States in 1899 and had just obtained his American citizenship on 28 May 1914.

Engineer William Frederick Ebeling poses here beside the decompression chamber installed aboard *Marie-Josephine*. (Ralph S. Blydenburgh photo album, author's collection)

A pair of divers, wearing the brand-new Siebe-Gorman helmets, are preparing to dive together. (Ralph S. Blydenburgh photo album, author's collection)

▲ Diver Henry Chinchen holding a cardboard model of a section of *Empress* on *Marie-Josephine*. (Mariners' Museum)

▶ A diver on the ladder on the side of *Marie-Josephine*, about to go down on the wreck. (Ralph S. Blydenburgh photo album, author's collection)

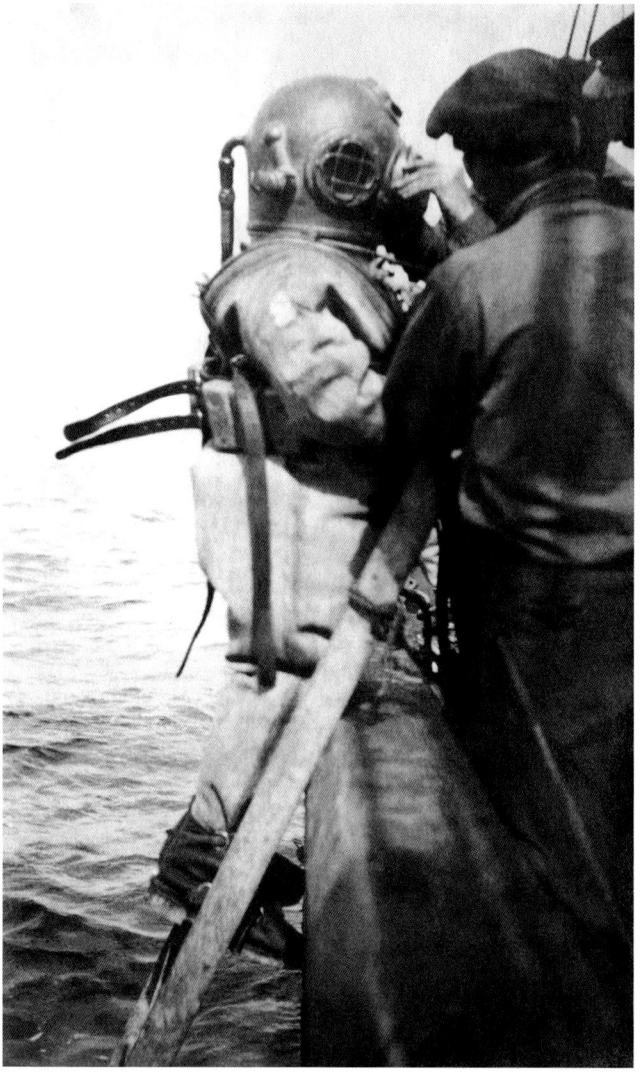

plans. Based on these, a cardboard model of the section of *Empress* where the valuables were located was made to prepare for the operation and to acquaint the divers with the route to be taken through the wreck.

The specie room was located amidships on the Upper Deck, and the passageway to get there from the opening on the port side of the hull was a working passageway where the saloon stewards would have had their quarters. While preparing the route through the ship, two things appeared obvious: several doors flanked the passageway that the divers would have to enter and, more importantly, two large passageways opened up on either side just before they would reach the door to the specie room. To prevent the divers from becoming disoriented and lost in the surrounding rooms or passageways, it was decided that all openings and doors except the door to the target hold would have to be sealed off inside the wreck. As it would probably take dozens of trips back and forth in this passageway for weeks, this preliminary step was essential. In addition to the cardboard model, the team of divers had to familiarise themselves with the configuration of the ship using various drawings.

Countless hours of planning, work and effort were invested in the operations. The team now included eight divers and more than a dozen assistants, sandhogs and engineers. While some divers were preparing to salvage the valuables, others continued to search every accessible section of the wreck for bodies of victims.

However, the changing and capricious natural conditions of the St Lawrence River estuary at this

ROBERT GREGG SKERRETT

The diagrams reproduced on the next page were prepared by Robert Gregg Skerrett, another fascinating character who revolved around Wotherspoon and his group. Skerrett was an engineer, lawyer, diver, photographer, marine artist and journalist. A personal friend of William W. Wotherspoon, he wrote several articles on the exploits of the Yankee Salvage Association between 1908 and 1915 and often travelled to the company's operations to report on them. He seems to have travelled to Rimouski himself in the summer of 1914 to attend part of the diving operations and he could even be responsible for some of the photographs taken on the spot. In the months that followed, he wrote about the salvage operations on *Empress of Ireland* in a number of newspapers and specialised magazines, including *Scientific American*, *Popular Mechanics* and *International Marine Engineering*, among others. While it was impossible to prove without a doubt that Skerrett was present in Rimouski, photographs in the album prove that he was on site with the Yankee Salvage Association a year later in Mexico. Jorge Acevedo, the Mexican Vice Consul in New York, had recommended the hiring of the company to the Mexican Government to salvage SS *Progreso*, a cruiser of the Mexican Navy. R.G. Skerrett, Ralph S. Blydenburgh and others all appear together in a number of photographs taken by Blydenburgh during that operation in Campeche, Yucatán, in May 1915.

Robert Gregg Skerrett is the man in the centre. This photo was taken by Ralph S. Blydenburgh in front of the Puerta de Tierra in Campeche, Yucatán. Jorge Acevedo, the Mexican Vice Consul in New York, is on the right. (Ralph S. Blydenburgh photo album, author's collection)

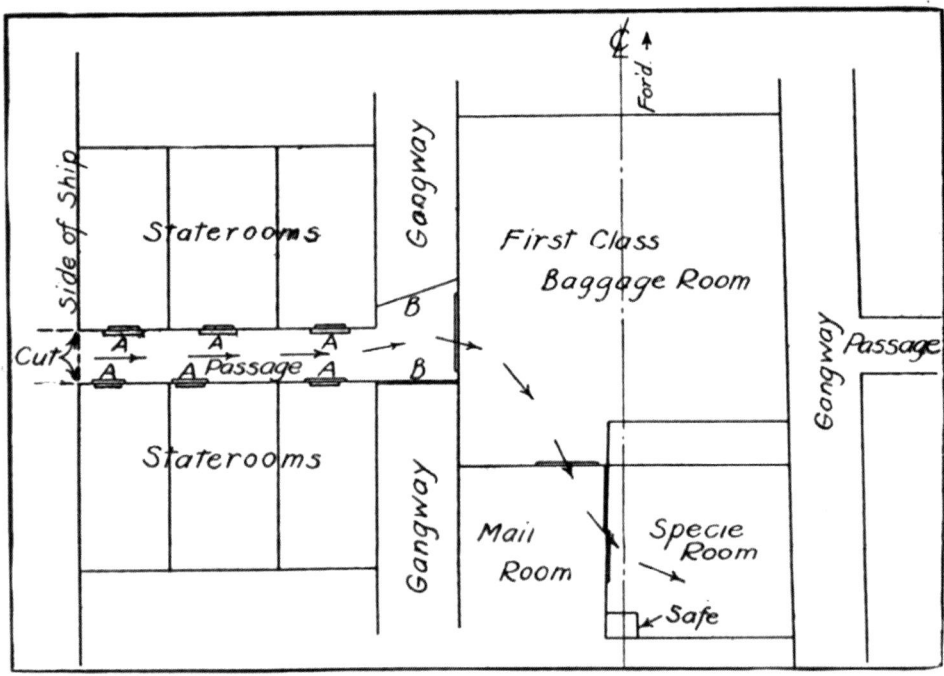

Fig. 1.—Plan of Part of Upper Deck of the *Empress of Ireland*

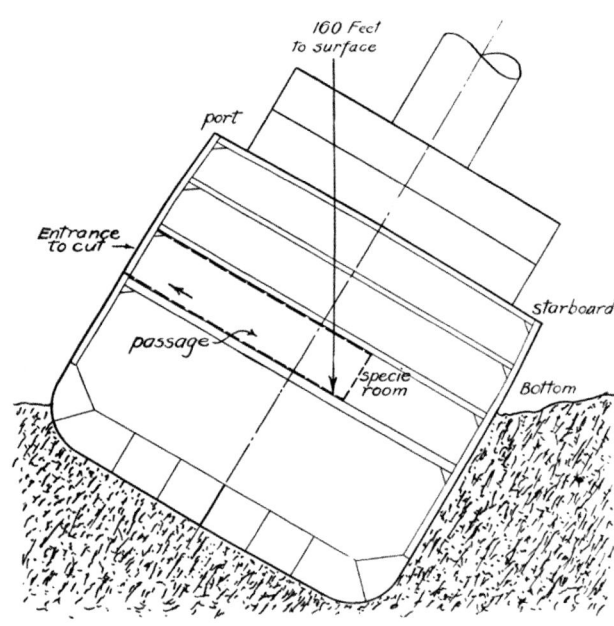

Fig. 2.—Diagram Showing Position of the Vessel

Plans showing the passageways used by divers to reach the specie room. In the sketch on the left, the letters A and B correspond to the openings that the divers had to block in order not to get lost in the wreck. The arrows show the path they would have to follow to remove the desired objects from the wreck. (*International Marine Engineering*, 1915)

location made it impossible to dive every day. Even when *Marie-Josephine* made it to the dive site, the river conditions had to be ideal for diving. Wotherspoon remained in charge of the work all through these few weeks and during this period he spent a lot of time studying the tides and currents on the surface and on the bottom at the wreck site. Wotherspoon called upon the advice and opinions of his friend and collaborator Robert Owen King, especially regarding his experiments to understand the currents and predict the best times for the dives and bringing up the valuables. King had mostly diverted his activities away from ship salvage, but remained interested in the experiments and he and Wotherspoon kept corresponding and collaborating.[22]

Wotherspoon was keen to ensure that his divers descended to the wreck in minimal current conditions on the surface, but especially on the bottom, to prevent them from tripping, being swept off their feet or simply to avoid making their job too difficult. One of the most important experiments he conducted was to measure the currents at different phases of the tides and at different depths. Towards the end of July, several days were devoted entirely to this exercise.

In order to measure and attempt to predict the movement of currents at different depths, Wotherspoon, with the advice of King and the help of his on-site team, designed small battery-powered electric lights that he could float and let adrift at different depths.

---

22 King remained involved in the marine industry and spent the few years immediately preceding the First World War working on experimental submarine and torpedo technology. (Michael F. Bardon, Galen R. Perras, & J. Graham Lindsay. *op. cit.*)

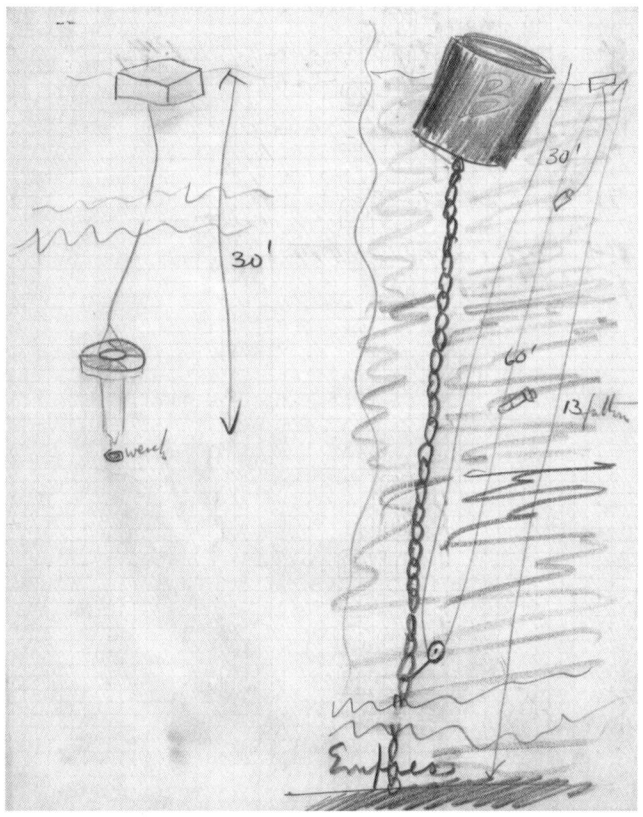

◀ Diagram drawn by Wotherspoon to show King how the lights are released along the 'bridge' buoy. (Library and Archives Canada/Exchequer Court of Canada fonds/59M-Exhibit P14)

▲ Photograph of the same installation in place. (Ralph S. Blydenburgh photo album, author's collection)

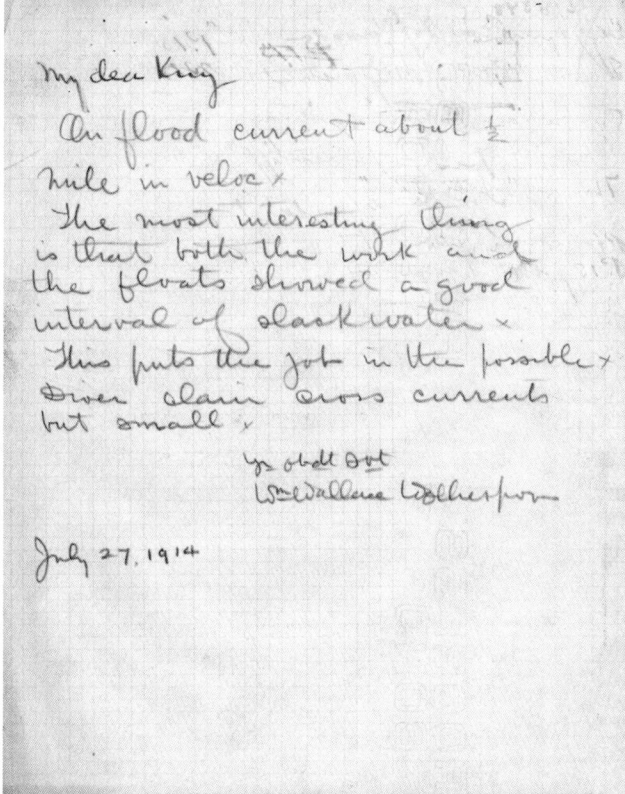

By using floats and weights that allowed the lights to remain vertical, the team could track their movements and measure the distance they travelled from the buoy attached to *Empress of Ireland*'s bridge at the centre of operations. Wotherspoon then measured the time elapsed between different distance marks and recorded the results. With floating lights released at depths of 30, 45 and 60ft, in addition to measurements taken directly on the surface, his estimates gave him a good understanding of tidal conditions. After several days of these experiments, Wotherspoon concluded that dives could only be made safely during short periods of slack water: the time between ebb and flood tides when surface currents are nearly zero. He continued to document the tidal movements for several weeks into August and maintained

▶ Letter from Wotherspoon to Robert O. King, dated 27 July 1914, about his currents and tides observations. (Library and Archives Canada/Exchequer Court of Canada fonds/59M-Exhibit P15)

close correspondence with Robert Owen King about his observations throughout the weeks of July.[23]

While these operations were taking place over the wreck, in Rimouski and Quebec City, two inquiries were concluding their work. Coroner Pinault's inquest in Rimouski, which began on the morning of 29 May, was adjourned on 30 May without a definitive conclusion. That inquest only heard witnesses from the rescue ships *Eureka* and *Lady Evelyn* and survivors from *Empress of Ireland*, since *Storstad*'s crew were still on their ship en route to Montreal. Not surprisingly, the preliminary conclusions, dated 30 May and signed by Pinault, were one-sided, suspecting 'criminal negligence' as a cause of death.[24] The inquest had initially been supposed to resume on 7 July, but by then the Mersey Commission of Inquiry was just about to conclude. Once again adjourned, the inquest was terminated officially on 18 July, without definitive conclusions. Coroner Pinault wrote to the Assistant Prosecutor of Quebec, 'No verdict was reached, the jurors arguing that there was a lack of evidence, not having been able to hear testimonies from the officers of the *Storstad*.'[25]

The Commission chaired by Lord Mersey had begun on 16 June and, during eleven days of hearings, heard sixty-one witnesses, to whom 7,847 questions were asked. Dozens upon dozens of documents were filed and reviewed by the commission, some of them especially produced for the hearings. In the end, the versions of events presented to the Commission of Inquiry by the crew members of the two ships were in many ways diametrically opposed and the Commissioners had great difficulty in deciding who

Alfred Toftenes (on the right), Chief Officer of SS *Storstad*, photographed on board the collier a few days after the collision with *Empress of Ireland*. (Guy D'Astous)

was right or wrong. The report was tabled on 11 July by Lord Mersey, who read the main conclusions at 10 a.m. in the Quebec City Courthouse. Less than six weeks after the sinking, the Commission placed greater blame on *Storstad*'s chief officer, Alfred Toftenes, who was on the bridge at the time of the collision, for having ordered the ship to turn to starboard in the fog and not waking up

---

23   The archives of the Exchequer Court in Ottawa keep a great number of documents relating to these experiments, including correspondence between King and Wotherspoon, tables of results, sketches and maps.

24   This dramatic preliminary finding was a way to open the door for a more formal investigation. (Archives Nationales du Québec in Québec City, E17, Fund of the Ministry of Justice.)

25   That letter is the official conclusion of the inquest, and shows that Coroner Pinault took the decision to close the inquest himself, without instructions from Quebec. (Archives Nationales du Québec in Québec City, E17, Fund of the Ministry of Justice.)

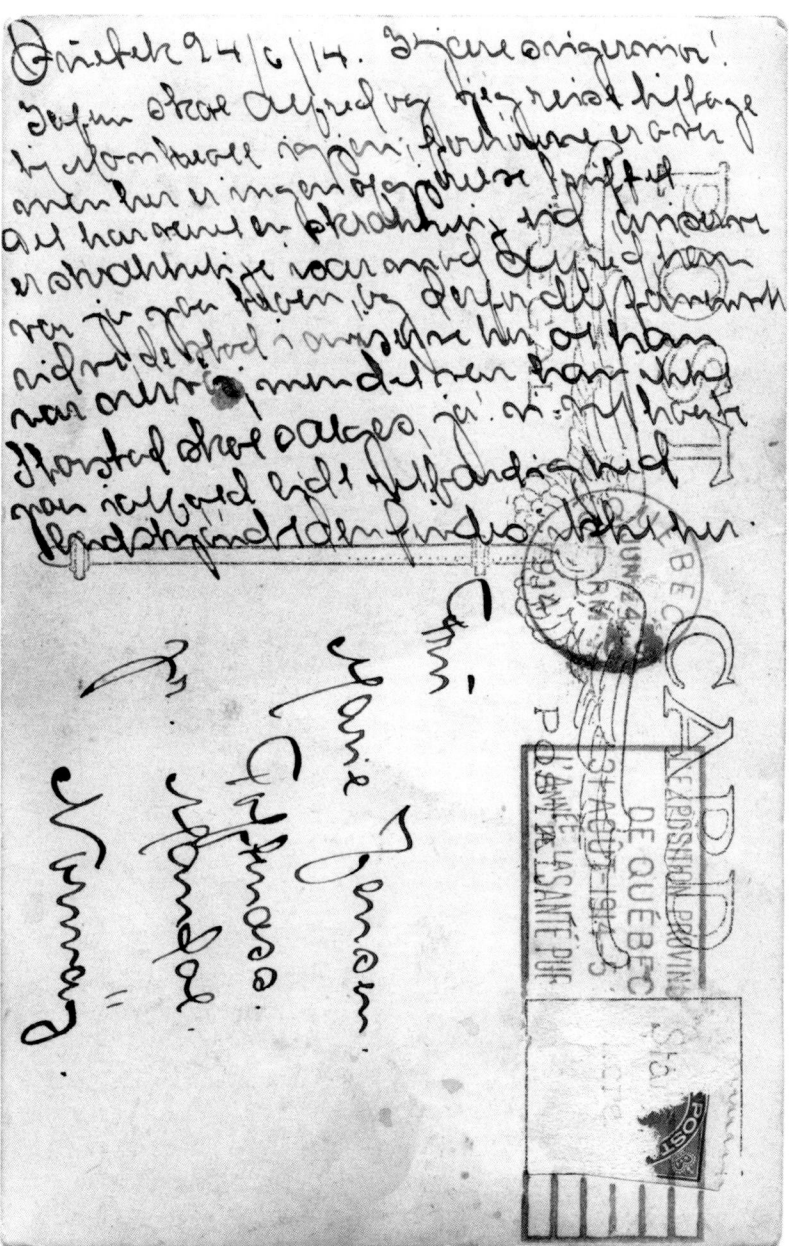

The postcard sent by Alfred Toftenes' wife. (Jan Hauge Nilsen/Toftenes family/NRK)

MULTIPLE CLAIMS: A LEGAL SAGA LASTING MORE THAN A DECADE

Even before the Commission of Inquiry completed its work, the Canadian Pacific Railway Company had *Storstad* legally seized to cover part of the losses and expenses incurred by the sinking. On 7 July, in Montreal, under court supervision, *Storstad* was sold at auction for $175,000, purchased by its former Norwegian owners acting through a local agent, Charles W. Cornell of Montreal.[1] SS *Storstad*, repaired in the next few weeks at the Davie Shipyard in Lévis, was quickly put back into service with the same crew. The amount of this sale represented only a mere fraction of the losses and expenses incurred by the Canadian Pacific Railway following the wreck. Including the estimated value of *Empress of Ireland* herself, the total amount claimed by Canadian Pacific was $2,406,822.59![2] The value of the resold *Storstad* was even less when one takes into account the invoices presented by the different entities involved in the rescue and salvage operations during 1914, including the Yankee Salvage Association, and the claims of the victims' families. The amount claimed from Canadian Pacific by the Yankee Salvage Association and the Quebec Wrecking and Salvage Association totalled $51,662.90. This total did not include the amounts for bullion claimed by the insurers and the amounts for mail claimed by the Postmaster General of Canada. In the Canadian courts, the matter of compensation and claims, insurance amounts and damages had only just begun and would continue until the end of the 1920s, without ever really resolving the difference between the total amount of claims and damages. In the end, most of the victims' families received only minor compensation in the best cases or, for the most part, nothing at all from the courts or the Canadian Pacific Railway.

1   The documents and minutes of the sale are kept in the Exchequer Court documents: LAC-BAC, Exchequer's Court, 59M.
2   According to the Bank of Canada's inflation calculator, this amount would be equivalent to over $64 million in 2024. This amount is for illustrative purposes only, as building a ship equivalent to *Empress of Ireland* today would obviously involve much more substantial costs.

his captain in fog, contrary to a standing order on the ship. For Mersey and his commissioners, the change of course of *Storstad* was the direct cause of the collision itself, although it was not the only cause. Captain Kendall could have passed *Storstad* from further away, giving the Norwegian collier more room to manoeuvre, and the commissioners also doubted Captain Kendall's version that his vessel was completely dead in the water at the time of the collision. However, in the same breath, the commission emphasised that the vessels would have met without an accident if neither of them had changed course in the fog. This is why Toftenes' order to his helm to turn *Storstad* to starboard in the fog was retained as the main cause of the accident.[26] The Commission also

26   In recent years, a number of commentators insisted that the inquiry presided over by Lord Mersey was biased in favour of the British steamship *Empress of Ireland*, some going as far as to elaborate conspiracy theories. It is interesting to note that even the lawyer representing *Storstad* did not think it was biased. In a letter dated 6 August 1914, Charles S. Haight wrote to Fin Koren, Norwegian Consul in Montreal: 'I met the members of the Court and the assessors frequently, during the two weeks of the hearings, and their attitude towards me was anything but hostile. I also met a number of Quebec judges and a large number of Quebec lawyers, and they were so outspoken in their resentment of anything that looked like a bias in favour of the Empress that, at times, I was actually embarrassed.' (National Archives of Norway, RA-S-1724 – Utenriksstasjonene, Legasjonen/Ambassaden i London, Da, L0486, 0021 – SJØ 22 D/S 'Storstad's kollisjon med 'Empress of Ireland', courtesy of Kjetil Saugestad.)

Storstad being repaired in the Davie shipyard dry dock, July 1914. (Musée Maritime du Quebec)

had to try to determine what caused *Empress* to sink so quickly and make recommendations to avoid such loss of life in the future.[27] The Commission therefore ended its work on this note, which led one Montreal daily French newspaper to say: 'At the end of this week, all traces of the terrible disaster will have disappeared: oblivion will take back what belongs to it.'[28] For the Norwegian crew of *Storstad*, this whole process was a difficult ordeal. Captain Andersen, Officer Toftenes and their families felt that they had been treated unfairly by the local media, especially, and also by the inquiry.

In late June, Alfred Toftenes' wife sent to her mother-in-law a postcard of the *Empress* victims' funeral procession in Quebec, on which she wrote:

> The newspapers are rude, especially with Alfred. He was on the bridge after all and is thus the most important witness. The newspapers wrote that he was nervous, but he was not. The Storstad will be sold. Yes! We hope for some decency, although it seems that this virtue is absent here. This is the funeral after the Empress. Yes! It's so sad. The newspapers at home are wrong too, I can tell you. We have to hope that the truth will come out one day. As you can imagine it was really terrible to sit and hear how Alfred was cross-examined by the best lawyers in the world, but they couldn't really bring him down. The truth, after all, is on his side.[29]

However, if for the rest of the world the *Empress* tragedy was more and more forgotten with each day that passed, in Rimouski history was still being written on a daily basis. On 25 July, the first divers who descended on the wreck noticed that *Empress* had shifted on the bottom of the river and that she had risen considerably. The wreck, since the sinking, had been lying on her starboard side, her masts at about 10 degrees to the river bottom. She then seemed to straighten up a little bit at a time. However, when the divers went down on 25 July, they found that her masts were now at an angle of about 40 degrees, which meant that the tip of the main mast was now only about 30ft from the surface. At this distance from the surface and considering that *Empress* could potentially continue to right herself, it was decided to have the Yankee Salvage Association cut off the bases of the masts and drop them to the bottom so the wreck would not be a hindrance to marine traffic.[30]

August

Wotherspoon's experiments confirmed that slack water, the time between tides when the river appeared to be still, was the ideal time to dive. The end of the ebb tide and low slack water provided the best conditions to carry out the work, as currents were at a minimum and divers needed to descend less deeply to reach the wreck. Several hours were therefore spent on *Marie-Josephine*, on the surface, waiting for the right tidal conditions.

---

27 These aspects of the inquiry would merit a longer and proper analysis. One can read a verbatim report of the inquiry and the final report by consulting: *Report and Evidence of the Commission of Inquiry into the Loss of the British Steamship 'Empress of Ireland' of Liverpool (O. No. 123972) through Collision with the Norwegian Steamship 'Storstad'*, Ottawa, Sessional Papers, Marine and Fisheries, 21b-1915.
28 'Tufetenes négligeant et fautif', *Le Devoir*, Montreal, 13 July 1914, p.8.
29 This postcard is reproduced on page 101. Source: Jan Hauge Nilsen/Toftenes family/NRK.
30 For some unknown reason, Yankee Salvage did not carry out this task. In fact, when divers rediscovered the wreck in 1964, they found that the masts were still upright, and documents consulted dating from 1968 and a testimony I was able to gather from divers of that early period show that the foremast was then pointing 40ft below the surface and the aft mast only 30ft: the same depths as in 1914!

Yankee Salvage crew with a gramophone on deck, 1910. (Ralph S. Blydenburgh photo album, author's collection)

This enlargement of the photo also shows a tiny puppy asleep on the arm of the man right next to the gramophone. Pets as mascots on board ships are a long-standing maritime tradition. (Ralph S. Blydenburgh photo album, author's collection)

According to Wotherspoon's notes, compiled over the course of the summer, *Marie-Josephine* sometimes spent up to forty-eight hours on the site, with experiments and dives sometimes done in the middle of the night. Given the obligation to dive only under good tidal and current conditions, the divers never stayed on the bottom for much more than thirty minutes at a time. One can thus imagine the impressive number of dives that these operations required.

The hours spent waiting over the wreck were used to check equipment, repair what needed to be repaired and study the configuration of *Empress of Ireland* with the model or plans. During some of the previous salvage

Yankee Salvage Association divers with a few assistants and Canadian Pacific Police Sergeant Irvine, waiting for the right tidal conditions to dive. Holding underwater telephone headsets in the foreground are divers Henry Charles Chinchen and William Lutz. (Mariners' Museum)

➤ A snow crab might be the next meal. (Ralph S. Blydenburgh photo album, author's collection)

➤➤ Snow crabs as pets! This one seems to be amusing a sandhog, on *Marie-Josephine*. (Ralph S. Blydenburgh photo album, author's collection)

operations in the United States, photos show the crew members using some of that off-duty time to take a few leisurely dives in their bathing suits, but the St Lawrence River waters were way too cold to practise this activity in Rimouski! Similarly, in 1910, over USS *Yankee*, the crew had brought a table gramophone to listen to music on board, but it does not seem that such a machine made the trip to Canada in the summer of 1914.

Here, it seems that fishing may have been one of the sources of distraction – and food – during moments of relaxation. Some of the photographs in Ralph S. Blydenburgh's album show that snow crabs seem to have earned the attention of the New Yorkers. These moments off, waiting for the tide, were certainly appreciated by the team, because the work was difficult and often gruesome. As of 31 July, at least sixty-one bodies had already been recovered from the wreck by the divers.[31] Without going very far into the lost ship, following Wotherspoon's orders not to penetrate the wreck, the divers opened the doors they found on the decks and in the hull and were able to explore some accessible compartments without too much risk. In doing so, the recovery of the bodies accelerated. On 3 August alone, diver Bargoni brought up seven bodies that he had recovered at the entrance of a first-class passage.[32] Diver Fred Rogall, for his part, brought up five bodies the same day. Some of the victims were identified as Catholics and during the first week of August the parish priest of Rimouski Cathedral ordered that the funeral bell be rung in honour of the dead from *Empress*.

On 3 August, *Empress of Britain*, the sister ship of *Empress of Ireland*, sailed up to Quebec City and, stopping in Rimouski to disembark the mail, brought

The time between dives still remained mostly devoted to planning the next descent and discussing the work ahead. (Ralph S. Blydenburgh photo album, author's collection)

aboard two divers from the Yankee Salvage Association team. This allowed them to take advantage of the eight-hour trip to study in greater detail than during their first visit the configuration of the passageways leading to the ship's vault.

---

31 It is unfortunately still impossible to establish the exact number of bodies that divers have brought up, since Coroner Pinault's archives have never been found. This figure as of 31 July comes from 'Des victims de l'Empress', *La Patrie*, Montreal, 31 July 1914, p.5.
32 Depending on the source, this surname appears written as 'Bargoni', 'Bargone', 'Barjoni' or 'Bergoni'.

Empress of Britain being repainted in camouflage grey while at sea, 9 August 1914. (Guy D'Astous)

As the divers boarded *Empress of Britain* in Rimouski, the wireless telegraph relayed the news to North America that Germany had declared war on Russia. In the early hours of 4 August, France in turn declared war on Germany, and a few hours later, Great Britain entered the war against Germany. Within hours, Europe was ablaze, and Canada, linked to Great Britain, was drawn into the conflict. This was *Empress of Britain*'s last peacetime voyage, and the ship was requisitioned by the British Admiralty to serve as a troop transport ship on her return to Britain. It would be almost five years before an *Empress* returned to the St Lawrence on a regular passenger crossing.

When the divers returned above the wreck to continue their preparations for recovering the safe and silver ingots, the world was a very different place. Following

The Yankee Salvage Association team poses on the deck of *Marie-Josephine* in Rimouski, with William Wallace Wotherspoon smiling in the foreground, on the left. In the foreground, one can recognise a Canadian diving helmet made by John Date of Montreal, which would have been worn here by Edward Lutz, the diver on the right in the photo, who is sporting a matching John Date breast plate. (Ralph S. Blydenburgh photo album, author's collection)

the plan patiently drawn up by Wotherspoon, one by one the divers carried out the delicate steps required to enter the passageway leading to the holds containing the silver ingots, safe and mailbags. Once the hull had been pierced and opened with the help of the 'Little David' hydraulic drill and winches on the surface, the passage had to be secured by marking out the right passageway in a precise manner. Dozens of dives, carried out by at least the same number of divers in rotation during July and August, enabled progress to be made inside the wreck, and by mid-August they were finally close to accessing the specie room itself.

It is difficult to fathom the efforts and difficulties associated with such underwater operations. The team was professional, well equipped and trained, but still, such complex work in the St Lawrence conditions was hard. There are indications that the divers themselves found the operations difficult, given the strong currents, cold water and poor visibility. Still, the photographs suggest a certain camaraderie right up until the end of the operations. In August, these men, who had been confined essentially to *Marie-Josephine* for two months out on the river, were smiling and had a swarthy complexion that breathed the sea and the fresh air.

At the end of a diving day, the equipment had to be inspected, cleaned and dried to prepare for the next day's dives. On some days, to dry the divers' suits, made of rubber and canvas, they were hung from the rigging of the main mast of *Marie-Josephine* or laid out on the decks of the schooner.

At the beginning of August, public attention was definitely focused on the conflict in Europe. The

THE DIVERS

On the British side, three divers from the HMS *Essex* team took part in the work in June 1914:
- **Keller, Alfred:** born on 20 October 1884. Was later in life working as a shoe repairman in Irthlingborough, England.
- **MacDonald:** first name unknown.
- **Whitehead, Wilfred:** born on 14 August 1889 in Huddersfield, England; joined the Royal Navy in 1907. He became a naval officer, then specialised in diving. He left the navy in 1921. He died in July 1962.

As for the commercial divers employed by the Yankee Salvage Association, a total of thirteen took part, in succession, in the operations of the summer of 1914. While some left traces, others are virtually unknown:
- **Bargoni:** first name and nationality unknown.
- **Bérubé:** first name unknown, mentioned only once in the sources.
- **Chinchen, Henry Charles:** born in Brighton, Sussex, England, in January 1875. He came to America in 1893, and was joined by his wife and children only in 1909. Father of six children, he died on 21 January 1920. He lived at 5715 3rd Avenue, Brooklyn. He had pale blue eyes and fair hair and he was 5ft 8in tall.
- **Cossaboom, Edgar Edward:** born on 26 June 1881, in Digby, Nova Scotia. He was 5ft 8in tall, with fair hair and blue-grey eyes. His father was Cornelius Cossaboom and his mother Rosetta Dooley. He left to work for Wotherspoon at the end of May 1914, arriving in New York on SS *Ralph* on 25 May 1914, and declared on his US entry document that his destination was 24 State Street, New York, the address of the Yankee Salvage Association offices. Cossaboom had been a high-seas fisherman out of Lubec, Maine, a few years earlier, and survived damage to his trawler, *Walter M. Young*, on 5 May 1910 near the Magdalen Islands. He drowned while diving on *Empress of Ireland* on 21 June 1914. His body was given to his brother for burial in the family plot on Gran Manan Island, New Brunswick.
- **Devine, Jack:** first mentioned on 8 July, and was still around on 19 August. In 1914, he held the world record for diving pressure (deep dive).
- **Evans:** first name unknown.
- **Jacobson, Selmer:** most probably the same person who, originally from Juneau, Alaska, was also a boat captain who was active on the west coast of Canada and Alaska a few years after 1914. He also participated in dives on the wreck of another ill-fated Canadian Pacific vessel, *Princess Sophia*.
- **Lutz, Edward William:** living in Jersey City, Lutz was recognised as one of New York's top divers. Lutz developed a particular expertise on *Empress* by helping to recover several bodies. Less than a year after the *Empress* dives, in April 1915, Lutz would make the front page of several American newspapers after recovering the bodies of two young people who had fallen into the waters of the Passaic River in New Jersey.
- **Rogall, Frederick:** born in Königsberg, Germany, on 6 April 1889, single. Acted as the tender holding Edward Cossaboom's cable at the time of his death. The following year, he was still employed by Yankee Salvage during the salvage of *Progreso* in Mexico. He was still a diver and worked for a salvage firm in 1917. Height 5ft 10in, dark hair, brown eyes, 162lb. He died on 14 June 1934.
- **Stuberg:** first name unknown.
- **Tuck, Edward J.:** born in Sudbury, Suffolk, England, in 1888, he had just immigrated to the US in 1914 when he was hired to take part in operations on *Empress of Ireland*. Married to Maud Sears and father of Edward Jr, Dorothy and John. In the summer of 1914, he declared as his own address the home of his friend, also a diver, Henry Chinchen, 5715 3rd Avenue, Brooklyn. He was 5ft 11in tall, with brown hair and grey eyes. He first immigrated to North America on 19 May 1913, arriving in Quebec City aboard *Ascania*. When amateur divers rediscovered the wreck of *Empress of Ireland* in the summer of 1964, Edward Tuck was still alive and sent them a letter of congratulations, recounting his memories of the dives of the summer of 1914.
- **Tremblay, Edmond and Thomas:** Edmond and his brother Thomas had already been diving for several years when Edmond dived on *Empress of Ireland*. A few years earlier, the two Tremblay brothers had participated in the search for valuable goods in a wreck in the Strait of Belle Isle. When Captain Joseph-Elzéar Bernier offered his services to refloat *Empress* a few days after the wreck, he said he could count on the Tremblay brothers. Originally from Jonquière, Quebec, Edmond was already a diver by 1896, and would continue in the trade for quite some time. In 1916, on the second anniversary of the sinking of *Empress of Ireland*, he appeared in some newspapers, announcing that he was forming a salvage company and would attempt to salvage copper from the wreck. Similarly, in 1918, he announced that he would refloat *Montmagny* if a patron advanced him the funds to do so. None of these operations came to fruition.
- **Wilson, Jack:** no further information was found.

Six of the divers pose on *Marie-Josephine*. (Ralph S. Blydenburgh photo album, author's collection)

various charitable actions, relief funds and subscriptions undertaken in the name of the victims became less active. While the crew of *Storstad* returned to their place on board and resumed carrying coal on the St Lawrence, traces of the tragedy became rarer, especially outside Canada.[33]

For the same reasons, August also saw the end of several initiatives to commodify the tragedy. Since the beginning of June, several people had, in their own way, commercially exploited the story of the disaster. This phenomenon had taken several shapes. Immediately after the funeral ceremonies held in Quebec City, movie theatres in town announced that they would be showing exclusive moving pictures of these events.[34] As early as 13 June, Quebec newspapers carried advertisements touting the excellent business opportunity of reselling souvenir postcards, posters or books on the tragedy.[35] Robert Deschêsnes, a photographer from Rimouski, had been a juror at the coroner's inquest, but he also took many photos of the aftermath of the disaster in that town and sold them as souvenir postcards throughout the province of Quebec. In fact, he might very well be

---

33 With war now declared, maritime traffic changed throughout the North Atlantic and, although Norway was officially neutral, *Storstad* did not escape the conflict. The ship was torpedoed by a German U-boat off the coast of Ireland on 8 March 1917, even though she was displaying large painted letters on her hull identifying her as a 'Belgian Relief Fund' ship.
34 *Québec Chronicle*, 12 June 1914.
35 The Logan Marshall book, *The Tragic Story of the Empress of Ireland*, was already advertised on the market as early as 10 June 1914, and an advertisement for it appears on p.10 of the *Québec Chronicle* of that date.

Divers' suits hanging from the mast of *Marie-Josephine* to dry. (Ralph S. Blydenburgh photo album, author's collection)

the originator of a number of the photographs in the Blydenburgh album.

Survivors and others directly involved in the tragedy or its aftermath gave extensive accounts of their experiences to reporters in the weeks following the sinking. Journalists printed these stories on the front pages on both sides of the Atlantic, and further afield; until August, in some markets, the story of *Empress* sold well. When the first survivors arrived in Great Britain, on the Allan Line's SS *Corsican*, pulling into Glasgow on 12 June, journalists literally swarmed the docks looking for stories. In an era when the news-hungry public demanded details, photos and even a 'feel' for the story, many people found ways to give the public what they wanted, sometimes making a good profit in the process. Two of the survivors even went so far as to participate in an entertainment stage show using special visual effects, fog machines and real wireless telegraphy equipment. Third-class passenger Elizabeth Kirtley, billed as 'the bravest woman of the lot', and first-class steward and member of *Empress*' Pierrot entertainment troupe, Whit Gray, performed *The St Lawrence Tragedy: The Loss of the Empress of Ireland* on stage, touring many cities in the United Kingdom.

This show had been put together by brothers Charles W. and John R. Poole. In the 1910s, the Pooles specialised in entertainment shows based on actual events, and made extensive use of complex scenography involving sound, visual and sensory effects, electrical equipment, tons of set material and sometimes even actors who had lived through the events being told. One of their most successful shows was *The Loss of the Titanic*, told in eight tableaux on stage. Presented as early as 1912, this theatrical event was still touring two years later, in 1914. When *Empress of Ireland* sank, *The Loss of the Titanic* was quickly adapted in the first few days after the sinking and the production company

A photograph taken by a Montreal family visiting the Rimouski area on their yacht in August 1914 shows the suits hanging on the mast to dry from a different angle. (Fetherstonhaugh family)

An advertisement for the stage show the *Loss of the Empress of Ireland*. (*The Era*, London, 15 July 1914)

Steam schooner *Marie-Josephine* with two divers on the ladders. (Mariners' Museum)

➤ The number of men needed to operate the air pumps was large, as can be seen here. (Ralph S. Blydenburgh photo album, author's collection)

➤➤ One of the large air tanks can be seen here, with white smoke billowing from the operating compressor, while two divers are on the bottom. (Ralph S. Blydenburgh photo album, author's collection)

began touring British stages with *The Loss of the Empress of Ireland*. The highly popular tour was only interrupted by the outbreak of the Great War in August 1914.[36]

The divers continued to descend on the wreck in pairs for the rest of the operations. In the order of priorities, recovering the safe was the first target. Once the main valuables hold was reached, the smaller specie room containing the safe was located a little distance aft. One of the main difficulties of this part of the task was to dislodge the safe from the special niche in which it was fixed. Armed with crowbars, the divers descended to the bottom, deep into the heart of the sunken *Empress*, to free the chest from its anchorage. In succession, the divers forced the safe until it was free.

---

36 Advertising for these different performances abound in British newspapers of the time. It is not known if anyone tried to claim the £500 that was promised to anyone who could prove that Kirtley or Gray were not actual survivors of the tragedy.

A large number of people patiently wait on the deck of *Marie-Josephine* for the safe to be raised. (Ralph S. Blydenburgh photo album, author's collection)

These three photos show in sequence the moment the purser's safe was raised from the deep on 19 August 1914. (Ralph S. Blydenburgh photo album, author's collection)

› A canvas bag is hoisted with a silver bar in it. (BANQ, fonds du Séminaire de Rimouski, Joseph Lepage, photographe)

›› A silver bar protrudes out of the canvas bag, now lying on the deck of *Marie-Josephine*. (Ralph S. Blydenburgh photo album, author's collection)

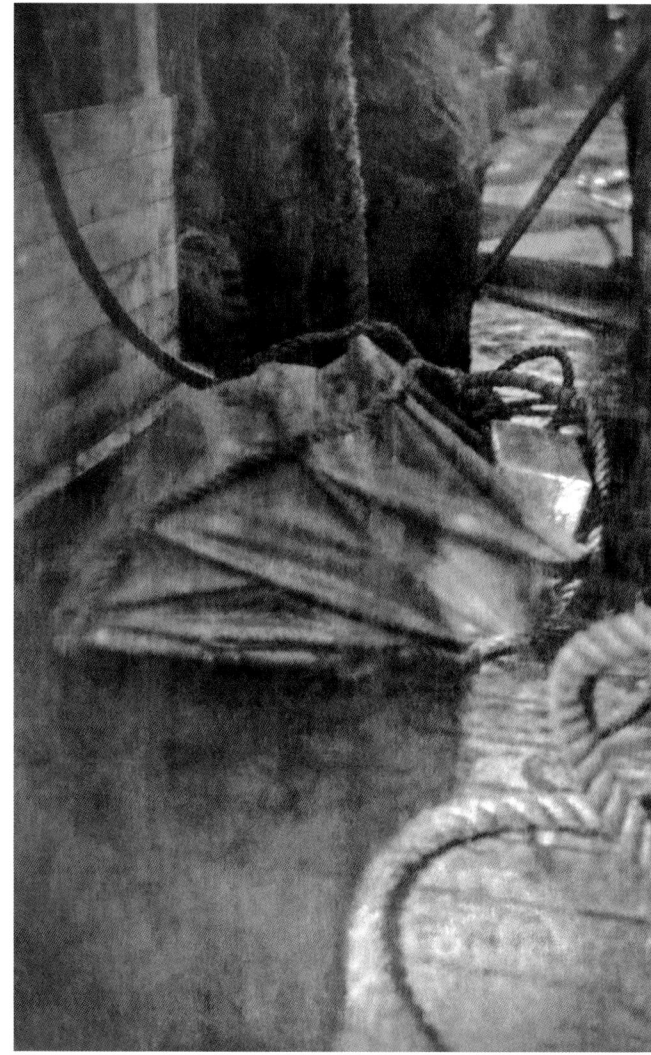

The regular hand pumps that supplied the divers with air required the strength of several men. Four men operated the cranks at the same time, and depending on the length of the dive, two or three groups of four men were often needed in rotation. When the underwater work was carried out deeper, the greater pressure in the water required more air pressure. The task was gruelling and constant. After the departure of the HMS *Essex* divers, who used only hand pumps, their use became less frequent, and in August they were discontinued altogether. The use of two divers at a time, the depth and duration of the dives and the need for compressed air to operate the underwater tools necessitated the use of a large number of steam compressors and a large compressed-air tank to replace the manual pumps.

◄◄ A diver coming back up from the wreck on a ladder on the side of *Marie-Josephine*. (Ralph S. Blydenburgh photo album, author's collection)

◄ Helped back on board the schooner, a diver needs a hand from the tenders to remove his equipment. (Ralph S. Blydenburgh photo album, author's collection)

After Cossaboom's death, some of the divers' equipment was adapted and modified to avoid a similar accident. For example, a notch was cut at the base of the air-inlet valve on all divers' helmets, so that a constant flow of air could pass through, even if a diver inadvertently closed the valve.

It was on 19 August that the men of the Yankee Salvage Association, after weeks of hard work and careful preparation, were finally ready to extract the safe from the wreck and bring it to the surface. As the event had been awaited for weeks, several people from Rimouski went to the site aboard *Marie-Josephine* to witness the exploit. Chains were attached to the huge safe by divers at the bottom of the river and the slow but steady ascent from the bottom to the surface was achieved by a steam winch on *Marie-Josephine*. The

Telegram announcing to the Postmaster General Office that the divers have reached the hold of postal bags in the wreck, 22 August 1914. (© Government of Canada. Reproduced with the permission of Library and Archives Canada (2024), RG3-C-1/Vol. 633, file 69265)

steam winch allowed a constant force to be applied to hoist the safe, to prevent it from being knocked loose. People in the crowd held their breath for several minutes as the steam winches were activated. When the large safe finally emerged from the river and swung out of the water, spilling all the water that had been inside over the schooner's deck, one of the chains slipped and the safe was inches away from dropping back to the bottom. When the winch operator finally managed to slide it over the boat, everyone gathered for the event burst out in joy and applauded the feat that had just taken place before their eyes.

This huge safe took on special significance for the Canadian Pacific Railway and its insurers, as survivors and families of the victims filed claims for several hundred thousand dollars in lost property, some claiming that their valuables had been stored in the purser's safe. When the safe was finally opened on 22 August 1914 at the Bank of Montreal on St Peter Street in the Port of Quebec City, its modest contents revealed just how exaggerated some of the claims had been.[37] This operation, by reducing the amount of claims and disproving fraudulent claims, would eventually pay for itself.

In the same hold as the safe were the 251 bars of silver that the insurers had mandated the Yankee Salvage Association to recover. Valued at over $150,000, the bars were being transported to banks in London, Great Britain.[38]

Recovering silver bullion was a time-consuming operation, given their sheer number and the capacity to bring them up, which was limited to just a few at a time. After descending into the vault, the divers slid one ingot at a time, weighing around 72lb each, into a large canvas bag pierced at the bottom, so that the water would drain out while still trapping the ingot inside. The bag was then hoisted to the surface. This sequence was repeated for days, until all the ingots were recovered.

Day after day over the wreck, divers descended in rotation. Concurrently with the silver ingots, the divers also started, from 22 August, the recovery of Royal Mail bags.[39] By 27 August, twenty-four bags had already been recovered and brought back to Rimouski to be processed.

September

When the divers finally managed to get all 251 bars of silver out of the hold of *Empress of Ireland* it was time to celebrate and everyone wanted to be photographed with the treasure, starting with the bosses of the operation.

The photo of R.S. Blydenburgh with the silver bullion was printed as a souvenir postcard as early as 1914. This

---

37   A complete list of the safe's contents can be found in Appendix C of *Forgotten Empress*, David Zeni, Devon, Halsgrove, 1998, pp.211–14.
38   This is equivalent to a little over $4 million in 2024, according to the Bank of Canada's inflation calculator.
39   *Empress of Ireland* was a Royal Mail Ship (RMS) and held a contract to transport mail between Canada and the United Kingdom.

▲▲▲ Ralph Stratton Blydenburgh, secretary of King & Wotherspoon Salvage, poses with some of the silver bars recovered from the wreck in August 1914. (Ralph S. Blydenburgh photo album, author's collection)

▲▲ William Wallace Wotherspoon, here on the right, also posed with some of the silver bullion on the deck of *Marie-Josephine*, accompanied by John McWilliams, the Mayor of Pointe-au-Père and superintendent of the pilot station. (Ralph S. Blydenburgh photo album, author's collection)

▲ Some of the divers and sandhogs are recognisable in this photo, which was published in a magazine in June 1915, but unfortunately it is not in Mr Blydenburgh's album, hence the poor quality. (*World's Advance*, June 1915)

◄ A large pile of silver bars, some of them with 'FINE 999' stampings. (Ralph S. Blydenburgh photo album, author's collection)

Two unidentified women posing with one hand on a silver ingot on the after deck of *Marie-Josephine* at Rimouski Wharf. (Ralph S. Blydenburgh photo album, author's collection)

has been published in almost every book on the history of *Empress of Ireland* since then, and used in most news reports on the wreck, without ever identifying Mr Blydenburgh until now.⁴⁰ It is quite remarkable that the image reproduced here is not only taken from the original, but that it was taken from Mr Blydenburgh's personal photo album.

Wotherspoon, who was in charge of the whole operation, must have felt a great sense of pride at such a result. Although the work was not yet completely over when these pictures were taken, it was clear to the whole team by then that their presence in Rimouski, which had lasted for more than three months, was coming to an end. Although there were still hundreds of bodies inside the wreck, divers had managed to get out 118 of them and it was becoming less and less possible to consider going any further.

Many of the crew also had their photographs taken near the silver ingots. The smiles on the faces of the team in these photos show how the professional, scientific and technical achievements of the summer of 1914 were also personal achievements for these men.

The safe had been salvaged under police surveillance and immediately sealed and brought back to Quebec City to the vault of a bank, to be opened under a very rigid judicial protocol. The silver bars, on the other hand, were recovered on an autonomous basis by the Yankee Salvage Association, which then had to take care of their protection before handing them over to the insurers, after an agreement on salvage fees. Before being transported to Quebec City to be stored in a bank, as was the case for the safe, the ingots were carried on *Marie-Josephine* and served as a trophy for their salvagers, as shown in the photo of the pile of ingots reproduced here.

These stacks of precious shiny metal bars made a lasting impression and photos even show people who were not part of the team having direct access to the loot. The accessibility of the bullion in the small town of Rimouski was really quite remarkable, especially since it had been escorted by armed guards when it had been carried from the mines of Cobalt, Ontario, to the Port of Quebec to be loaded on *Empress of Ireland* just a few months earlier.

---

40 He was even wrongly identified a few times, including by the professor of local history at Rimouski College, Father Lionel Pineau, who had identified the man in this photo as Alphonse Couillard, former postmaster at Rimouski. (Lionel Pineau, 'Le Naufrage de l'*Empress of Ireland*', *Revue d'histoire du Bas-Saint-Laurent*, Vol. 1, No. 3, December 1974, p.6.)

On 10 September, the Canadian Salvage Association, the Yankee Salvage Association's Canadian subsidiary, was officially incorporated by letter patent under the leadership of Lorne C. Webster of Montreal. William Wallace Wotherspoon was obviously one of the directors, but also among the patrons were Noël Belleau of Lévis and William Quarrier Stobo, a Quebec City businessman.[41] The company was formally incorporated so that it could continue to offer its services as a Canadian company and not just as a subsidiary of an American company. Once incorporated, the Canadian Salvage Association officially replaced the Yankee Salvage Association as a contractor for their Canadian operations and could more easily obtain public contracts for salvage operations and the loading and unloading of ships in the St Lawrence. It is with this legal entity that Wotherspoon continued the work on *Empress of Ireland* and the procedures to obtain compensation for the work would be initiated.

This became central in the weeks that followed. The Canadian Pacific Railway Company paid all the bills presented to them for the salvage of the safe, the diving equipment, the raising of the bodies of victims and even for the testimony of Wotherspoon at the Commission of Inquiry. But the same was not true for the other parts of the salvage contract, for the silver bullion and for the mail. For the mail matters, the arrangement with the responsible federal department was that the government would pay the associated costs incurred and compensations in proportion with the value of the mail recovered, subject to the complete success of the operation.

On 16 September, Wotherspoon announced that he had completed operations after the last accessible mailbag was brought up. Around 118 bodies, the purser's safe, 251 bars of silver and 319 mailbags containing more than

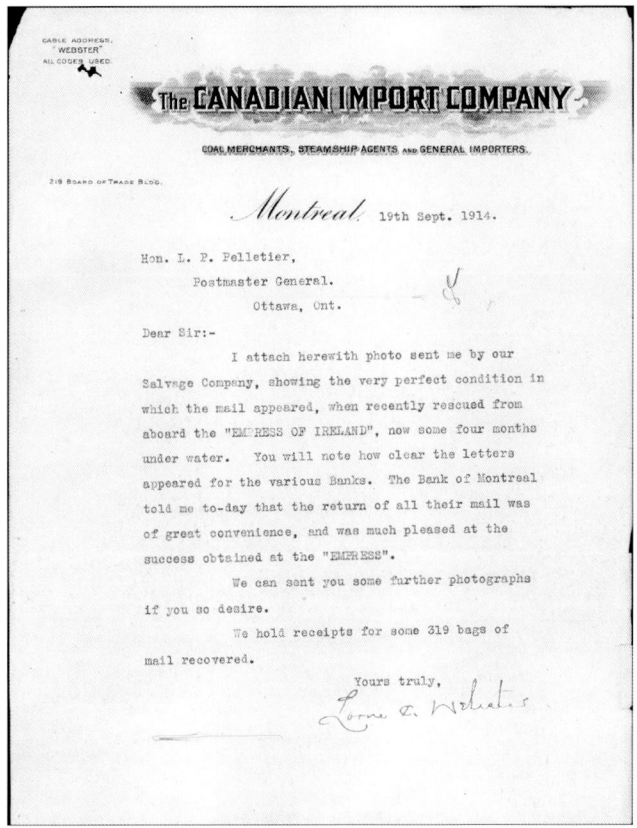

The telegram sent to the Postmaster General Office in Ottawa to announce the success of the mail salvage operation. (© Government of Canada. Reproduced with the permission of Library and Archives Canada (2024), RG3-C-1/Vol. 633, file 69265)

2,100 miscellaneous letters and hundreds of registered documents were brought to the surface.[42] The photo on the next page shows some of the letters pinned to a wall in Rimouski Post Office, where they were drying. A copy of it was sent by Lorne C. Webster, on behalf of the Canadian Salvage Association, to the Postmaster General on 19 September 1914 to prove the excellent condition of the recovered letters. The condition of the mail matters put the Canadian Salvage Association in a good position to initiate a discussion with the minister about the monetary compensation expected for the

---

41   *Quebec Official Gazette*, Province of Quebec, Vol. XLVI, No. 38, 19 September 1914, p.2322.
42   The total number of mailbags brought to the surface was 318 intact and one torn and damaged. (LAC-BAC, RG3-C-1, Vol. 633.)

The photograph used by the salvage company to prove the legibility of the mail recovered from the wreck. (Ralph S. Blydenburgh photo album, author's collection)

recovery of the mailbags. The mission was a success but the amount of compensation for the divers' work had not yet been agreed upon with the government, since it depended on the value of salvaged mail, and that value depended on its condition, legibility and the possibility of processing it to its final destination.

The photo showed that the addresses on the envelopes, even after several months underwater, could still be read. The salvagers were claiming a total of $15,000 from the Crown for the recovery of the mail and insisted in their correspondence that the feat would prove to the world that mail carried by the Royal Mail on the St Lawrence River was safe and could be recovered and forwarded under any circumstances. The reputation of the Canadian postal authorities was at stake and Lorne C. Webster knew how crucial and lucrative this service was to the government. Despite this, it took months of lobbying and correspondence before the government finally paid a portion of the $15,000 claimed to cover the Canadian Salvage Association's expenses. In its defence, the Postmaster General's Office wanted to ensure that the value of the mail items being reassembled and forwarded to their destination was correct. In order to do so, all the salvaged mailbags were given to the postmaster of Rimouski, who was in charge of opening them and drying the letters.

Once the letters were dry, they were sent for processing to the Dead Letter Office in Ottawa, which then returned the mail to the sender, when possible, who could decide whether or not to redirect it to the original destination. Before the letters were redirected, the General Delivery Office marked each envelope with a stamp that read 'Recovered by divers from wreck of S.S. Empress of Ireland'.

At the very end of the salvage operations, in mid-September, some of the team posed for posterity on the

▲ Letters placed on a flat surface to dry at Rimouski Post Office. (Canadian Museum of History, 2012-H0018.259)

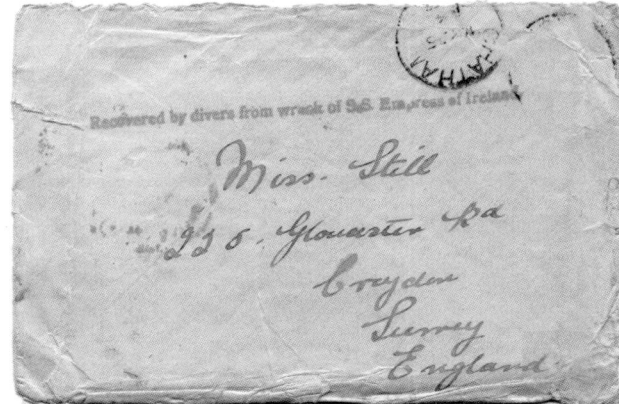

◀ A letter recovered by divers. (Author's collection)

The New York salvage team at the end of the operations in Rimouski. Ralph S. Blydenburgh (front row, second from left) is seated in front of sergeant Irvine of the Canadian Pacific police. (Ralph S. Blydenburgh photo album, author's collection)

deck of *Marie-Josephine*, their complexions tanned after months out on the river. The team, for the most part, remained in Rimouski for a few more days to conclude the operations by removing some of the equipment and diving gear from the site.

On 18 September, another collision in the St Lawrence River resulted in the loss of a ship and casualties. CGS *Montmagny* was struck in the middle of the night by the coal carrier SS *Lingan* just off Isle-aux-Grues, resulting in fourteen casualties, even though she sank in shallow waters. In a strange twist of fate, she was the same vessel that had been employed two years before to sail to the wreck site of the *Titanic* disaster to try to recover victims' bodies. *Montmagny*'s masts were still visible above the surface. As the dive team under Wotherspoon's direction was still in Quebec, they were asked to go to the scene of the accident and attempt to recover the bodies of the victims. Their first dive on *Montmagny* was on 25 September. Edward Tuck descended to the wreck and managed to find his way

CGS *Montmagny*'s masts and the top of her funnel are visible at the surface after her sinking. *Marie-Josephine* is moored over the wreck. (Fonds Lucienne Masson, Parks Canada collection in Quebec)

near the victims' quarters, but was unable to recover any bodies at that time.[43]

After this date, the team broke camp in Rimouski and headed back to New York, except for Wotherspoon and Blydenburgh, who remained in Quebec City at the Château Frontenac Hotel to see to the settlement of the silver bullion case in court. The Canadian Salvage Association had to appear before Judge Adolphe Basile Routhier to support its case against the insurance companies, who were claiming the silver ingots recovered from the wreck of *Empress*.[44] Canadian Salvage refused to hand over the silver without a guarantee that it would be paid for the recovery. The 251 silver ingots were placed in the vaults of a Quebec City bank. They were valued at $150,000, but the Canadian Salvage Association claimed $100,000 in fees for the diving work required to recover them. Complex legal procedures then began, which would drag on for years.

---

43 CGS *Montmagny* was a lighthouse station tender and government assistance vessel. Diving continued well into October at the *Montmagny* wreck, and some bodies were later recovered or found ashore. Her story was the subject of a few articles, a documentary and a book in French (Hubert Desgagnés, *C'était en 1914, l'année des charbonniers, Naufrage du C.G.S. Montmagny, le 18 septembre 1914*).

44 It is the same Basile Routhier who, a few years earlier, had written the lyrics of the French Canadian patriotic piece that would become Canada's national anthem, 'O Canada!'.

CONCLUSION: AUTUMN 1914

Canada followed Great Britain into the First World War in August 1914. When the first contingent of Canadian forces left for the European theatre of war, it was by a convoy of liners converted into troop carriers. This convoy of thirty-two ships and a number of armed escorts, carrying 33,000 men who had been trained for weeks at a camp in Valcartier, left Quebec City on 3 October 1914. This 'Canada's Great Armada', as it was named in the papers, practically sailed over the site of the sinking of *Empress of Ireland* on 4 October. For the first time in a few weeks, after a very busy summer, the silence that had settled over the site was broken.[1]

Wotherspoon had time to participate in another salvage operation in November, when Red Star Line's *Zeeland* had to be dislodged from a muddy promontory on Lake Saint Pierre, near Sorel, Quebec.[2]

That same month, in Admiralty Court, the Canadian Salvage Association pleaded its case against the silver bullion insurers. The company outlined the expenses it had incurred, the risks it had taken and argued that the salvage operation had cost the life of a diver and was only successful because of the unique expertise of Wotherspoon and his men. The insurers, on the other hand, argued that the company could be compensated for the expenses incurred, but could not claim any additional costs because it had chosen to take all these risks. In March 1915, Judge Routhier ruled in favour of the Canadian Salvage Association and awarded it reimbursement for its expenses, plus one-fifth of the value of the silver ingots. It was not the $100,000 the company had originally asked for, but nearly $60,000, which was almost double the amount of its expenses for the salvage operation alone. Above all, Judge Routhier stated that the case law and the spirit of the law supported the idea that compensation to salvors must be high in order to encourage the very idea of salvage at sea and to encourage contractors to take risks to salvage vessels or their cargo in case of a sinking.

While Ralph Stratton Blydenburgh finally returned to New York by boat, rounding the tip of the Gaspé Peninsula, Wotherspoon remained in Quebec City for some time. The United States had not yet entered the war, but the effects of the conflict in Europe were already being felt in trade and industry. As soon as the work in Rimouski was completed in the summer of 1914, many specialised newspapers and scientific magazines reported on the exploits of the Yankee Salvage Association on *Empress of Ireland*. Articles, sometimes abundantly illustrated, were published until at least the winter of 1915–16 to tell in great detail the success of this risky operation.

In May 1915, a rumour picked up by some Quebec newspapers suggested that Wotherspoon was returning to the St Lawrence with his team of experts to refloat

---

1 Some mentions of *Empress of Ireland* found their way into the correspondence of soldiers sailing near the wreck site and indicate that the tragedy was most probably mentioned aboard ships passing near Pointe-au-Père. One example is this letter by soldier Charlie Thicke dated 9 July 1915: 'Thursday, June 10, left Montreal with grand send-off. Had 1,500 on board. Had good day down St Lawrence, arriving in Quebec that night, and was inspected by the Duke of Connaught. Friday got out to sea, passing where the str. Empress of Ireland went down.' (Quoted in the 'Canadian Letters & Images Project' from the Canadian War Museum, canadianletters.ca/content/document-2408.)

2 This salvage job also made the news at the time, as the techniques employed were again quite innovative. See: Robert Gregg Skerrett, 'Floating a Stranded Ship on Air, Refloating the Steamship Zeeland', *Scientific American*, Vol. 112, No. 4, 23 January 1915, p.84.

Empress of Ireland. The reality was quite different. When Wotherspoon returned to the St Lawrence in the spring of 1915, it was to begin setting up his team near Baie-Trinité, an isolated village on the north shore of the river, to refloat the cargo ship SS *Hendonhall*, which had been grounded on the rocks since November 1914. Another difficult refloating, and another success.³ Wotherspoon had an outstanding reputation, but the war caught up with him, and with the United States entering the conflict, William Wallace Wotherspoon had to serve. Appointed a naval lieutenant, he spent the last year of the war in France, in charge of salvage operations on the Atlantic coast.

The diver Edmond Tremblay, who had participated in the 1914 salvage operations, set up his own salvage and diving company in 1916, with the idea of salvaging the wreck of *Empress of Ireland*. His project would never see the light of day and the giant wreck would remain essentially undisturbed and forgotten for fifty years, until the wreck was rediscovered in the summer of 1964. That year, a small group of amateur scuba divers from the Gatineau area of Quebec rediscovered the wreck with the help of some people from Rimouski. Even while the Great War was raging and the rest of the world slowly forgot about the tragedy of the St Lawrence, in that town, *Empress of Ireland*, lying on the riverbed a few kilometres off the coast with around 700 victims still trapped in her carcass, was still remembered.

The Red Star Line SS *Zeeland* aground near Sorel, Quebec, November 1914. (Ralph S. Blydenburgh photo album, author's collection)

The flotilla used to refloat *Zeeland* under the instructions of W.W. Wotherspoon. CGS *Lady Grey* and *Lord Strathcona* were among the boats used. (Ralph S. Blydenburgh photo album, author's collection)

---

3   Again, the feat was the subject of a number of articles in magazines at the time. For example: Robert Gregg Skerrett, 'The Refloating of the Hendonhall', *International Marine Engineering*, Vol. XXI, No. 1, January 1916, pp.26–27.

APPENDIX: EXTRA IMAGES FROM THE ALBUM

Ralph Stratton Blydenburgh documented the salvage operations in which he was involved from 1908 to 1917. In his album, he collected, organised and pasted more than 500 photographs that he had taken himself or got from other photographers who had been to the operation sites, from Newfoundland to Mexico. Blydenburgh seems to have been interested as much in the technical feats he was contributing directly to as he was in the cities and villages these contracts allowed him to visit. His photo album also gives exceptional access to the daily lives of these divers and sandhogs, how they lived and passed the time, while working in these extremely dangerous conditions. The following photographs, most of them unique and never before published, are a selection from the Blydenburgh album taken on other salvage operations between 1908 and 1917.

All images in Appendix from the Ralph S. Blydenburgh photo album, author's collection.

After *Yankee* sank in deeper waters, the salvage company prepared to try and refloat her for a second time. Here, two divers all dressed up are being carried by smaller craft to the wreck.

APPENDIX: EXTRA IMAGES FROM THE ALBUM   129

Bringing a large metal shaft over the wreck to create an airtight lock to allow sandhogs to descend in the pressurised hull.

Adjusting the lock over the wreck.

Yankee is raised.

Yankee's bow and bridge emerge from the deep ... just to sink again a little later.

Waiting for the right time to dive, 1908.

APPENDIX: EXTRA IMAGES FROM THE ALBUM 131

Ralph S. Blydenburgh enjoying a swim around the *Yankee* wreck, 1908.

◄ William Wallace Wotherspoon (in the middle, back) holding a notepad and pen, examining USS *Nero* from a lifeboat.

▼ The auxiliary collier USS *Nero*, grounded on the rocks at Brenton's Reef, near the entrance to Narraganset Bay, Rhode Island, USA, July 1909.

APPENDIX: EXTRA IMAGES FROM THE ALBUM   133

The refloated USS *Nero* brought in to dry dock for repair by the Yankee Salvage Association/Arbuckle Wrecking Company, December 1909.

Some of the damage to USS *Nero* and temporary repairs made by the wreckers.

▲ After the successes of multiple ship salvage, John Arbuckle decided to purchase a few ships to create a wrecking fleet, among which was the very famous SS *Roosevelt*, the ship built especially for captain Robert Peary's expedition to the North Pole a few years prior.

▶ December 1910 and January 1911: cold and snow did not stop the crew from working on site.

▲ SS *Roosevelt*, purchased in the summer of 1910, was refitted for wrecking purposes, having one mast removed and sections reinforced.

▲ In 1910, the crew was back at the *Yankee*, using *Roosevelt*, this time to salvage part of the wreck and destroy and remove what was left of her.

APPENDIX: EXTRA IMAGES FROM THE ALBUM 135

The collier SS *Glace Bay* aground in Newfoundland, May 1913. A rare occasion when the ship could not be saved: a storm pounded at her and she broke in half before the salvage attempts could begin.

SS *Bürgermeister Hachmann* burned and sank at the dock in Brooklyn, New York, and was later refloated in September 1913.

◀ In September 1913, SS *Penn* of the Ericsson Line caught fire while at her mooring in the Port of Philadelphia, Pennsylvania. The amount of water used to fight the blaze made her sink, and the decision to refloat her was taken swiftly.

▲ The contract was executed, but not without great difficulty: it took forty-nine days and seven unsuccessful attempts before SS *Penn* could finally be raised and towed to be scrapped. Here a large crowd is watching one of the attempts to raise the wreck.

◀ SS *Penn*, finally refloated, is towed away.

APPENDIX: EXTRA IMAGES FROM THE ALBUM 137

Amid political and social unrest, in March 1915, the sole ship of the Mexican Navy, SS *Progreso*, was blown up by a group of rebels while blockading the port of the same name on the Yucatán Peninsula. The blast killed a dozen people and caused the ship to sink on a sandbar.

The Mexican Government of Venustiano Carranza gave a contract to the Yankee Salvage Association to try to refloat *Progreso*. Engineers Wotherspoon (second row, third from left) and Ebeling (middle, white shirt and arms crossed) pose here with part of their team on the deck of the wrecking tug SS *Forward*.

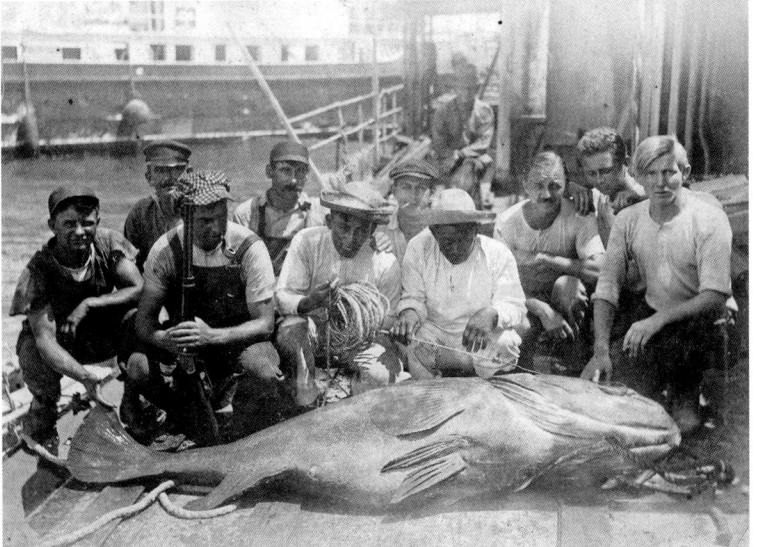

The heavy waves at that location were already making the job difficult, but the sharks and giant fishes of the area made it even worse. To protect the men, the salvage team built cages in which divers could descend.

Progreso, successfully refloated, was towed to Veracruz for permanent repair.

Right after the *Progreso* was refloated, the team sailed back to New York and then up to the St Lawrence to work on refloating SS *Hendonhall*, aground at Baie-Trinité, Quebec.

SS *Lord Strathcona*, now sporting a large Quebec Salvage & Wrecking Co. sign on her bridge, joined in on the effort with local men and equipment.

APPENDIX: EXTRA IMAGES FROM THE ALBUM 139

Divers work in pairs, as on *Empress of Ireland*, this time to make temporary repairs to the hull of *Hendonhall*.

Some of the numerous unidentified ships in trouble in the photo album.

ACKNOWLEDGEMENTS

In the course of this research, conception and writing, several people contributed, each in his or her own way, to making this book possible. These people have played an important role and I would like to thank them.

Sébastien Hudon, whose lucky find and instinct ultimately led to this project; Jeffrey Blydenburgh and Christopher Harlow, for having so generously welcomed a stranger from Quebec into the history of their family; Amy Rigg and Jezz Palmer and the rest of The History Press; Serge Lambert and Caroline Roy, from the publisher GID; Guy D'Astous, whose passion for *Empress of Ireland* is a great motivation; Serge Guay and Annemarie Bourassa, for their communicative and encouraging enthusiasm for some of my crazy projects and for decades steadily steering the Musée de la mer/Site historique maritime de la Pointe-au-Père through both calm and rough seas; Hélène Théberge for her support, collaboration and backing; my friend and artist extraordinaire Yves Bérubé; Alain Franck, for his support and advice; Jean Cloutier; Levi Rourke; Nicolas Haché; Tom Lynskey; J. Kent Layton; Amos Mayhugh; Alex Moeller; Kjetil Saugestad; Eve Lazarus; Guillaume Marsan; Pat Whitehead; Mike Babiski; Charles Dagneau; Rick Nelson; Ron Millar; the Salvation Army of Canada; Sarah Puckitt; Galen Perras; Michael Bardon; Graham Lindsay; Catherine Fetherstonhaugh; Derek Grout; David Zeni; Samuel Côté; Jean-Pierre Vallée; François Rousseau; (the late) Ian Kinder and Penny Vermeulen; Geoff Whitfield; Pierre Champagne and the Lower Canada Historical Society; Yves Tremblay; Robert Jourdain; Mike Poirier; (the late) David Creighton; Roxane Julien-Friolet, Martin Debofle, Raphaël Cousineau and the rest of the SHMP team; Renée Houde; Réal Lessard; George McNeil; Langis Dubé; Dany St-Cyr; Simon Pelletier; Gareth Abel; Andrew Gegenheimer; David Skinner; Joe Saward; Hugh Ferguson; Alain Vézina.

On a more personal note, thank you to my sweetheart, Marie-Sophie Villeneuve, for her support and encouragement, even when I thought the world had come to an end while waiting for the photo album to be found by the shipping company.

Thank you also to my parents, the first audience of all my historical flights since childhood.

BIBLIOGRAPHY

Archives

National Archives of Canada
Exchequer Court, *Empress of Ireland* Inquiry, R1191-24-3-E, RG42-B-3.
Empress of Ireland, Salvage of Cargo, RG42-B-1, Vol. 232, File 35762.
Salvage of Mails, etc. from wreck of the *Empress of Ireland*, RG3-C-1, Vol. 633, File 69265.

Archives Nationales du Québec
Correspondances avec le Procureur général du Québec (E17).

National Archives of Norway
Foreign Affairs, 0021 – SJØ 22 D/S 'Storstad's kollisjon med Empress of Ireland'.

Newspapers

La Patrie, Montreal, Quebec, Canada.
La Presse, Montreal, Quebec, Canada.
Le Peuple, Montmagny, Quebec, Canada.
Le Progrès du Golfe, Rimouski, Quebec, Canada.
Le Soleil, Quebec City, Canada.
New York Daily Tribune, New York City, USA.
The Gazette, Montreal, Quebec, Canada.
The New York Times, New York City, USA.
The Québec Chronicle, Quebec City, Canada.
The Standard, Montreal, Quebec, Canada.
The Sun, New York City, USA.

Periodicals

Carter, C.F., 'Compressed Air Saves Wrecks', *Technical World Magazine*, Vol. X, October 1908, pp.136–43.
——, 'Science to Save Wrecks', *Sunday Magazine*, 7 July 1907, p.8.
Case, Henry Jay, 'The "Sand-Hogs" and the Ship', *Harper's Weekly*, Vol. LIII, No. 2727, New York, 27 March 1909, pp.6–7.
Coppin, Clayton A., 'John Arbuckle: Entrepreneur, Trust Buster, Humanitarian', *The Freeman, Ideas on Liberty*, Vol. 40, No. 5, 1 May 1990, pp.192–96.

December 1917, near Baton Rouge, Louisiana, the team of divers pose while working on refloating SS *Gut Heil*, which sank in 1913. A lot of these men were also in Rimourski in the summer of 1914. (Ralph S. Blydenburgh photo album, author's collection)

Perras, Galen Roger, et al., 'R.O. King: The Professional Odyssey of a Practical Canadian Engineer', *The Northern Mariner/Le Marin Du Nord*, 18(2), 2008, pp.85–118.

Richards, Frank, 'Salvage Operations on *Empress of Ireland*', *Compressed Air Magazine*, November 1914.

Skerrett, Robert Gregg, 'A Notable Achievement in Deep-Sea Salvage', *The World's Advance*, Vol. 30, No. 6, June 1915, pp.765–70.

——, 'A Remarkable Salvage Operation Which Rubber Made Possible', *The India Rubber World Magazine*, 1 January 1915, pp.189–92.

——, 'Floating a Stranded Ship on Air, Refloating the Steamship Zeeland', *Scientific American*, 23 January 1915, p.84.

——, 'How Air Fight Fire and Water', *St Nicholas Magazine*, Vol. XLII, No. 10, August 1915, pp.899–905.

——, 'Modern Marine Salvage and its Potentialities, Raising Hundreds of Sunken Ships by Scientific Methods in Which Compressed Air Undoubtedly Will Play a Vital Part Will Develop an Entirely New Industry', *Compressed Air*, Vol. XXV, No. IX, September 1920, pp.9777–86.

——, 'Notable Salvage Work Upon the "*Empress of Ireland*"', *Scientific American*, 9 January 1915, p.49.

——, 'Salvage Work on the *Empress of Ireland*, A Distinct Advance in Deep-Water Salvage Achievements – Methods Employed and Difficulties Overcome', *International Marine Engineering*, Vol. XX, No. 2, February 1915, pp.60–62.

——, 'Salvage Work on Sunken "*Empress of Ireland*"', *Popular Mechanics Magazine*, April 1915, Vol. 23, No. 4, pp.482–83.

——, 'Salvage Work on Sunken "*Empress of Ireland*"', *The Labor Digest*, Vol. 7, April 1915, p.39.

——, 'The *Bavarian* Floated by Air', *The American Marine Engineer*, Vol. 1, No. 12, December 1906, p.11.

——, 'Salvage Operations on the *Empress of Ireland*', *Compressed Air Magazine*, Vol. XX, No. 2, February 1915, pp.7499–500.

——, 'The Refloating of the Hendonhall', *International Marine Engineering*, Vol. XXI, No. 1, January 1916, pp.26–27.

——, 'The Salvage and Repair of the Steamship "*Royal George*"', *Scientific American*, 26 July 1913, p.64.

Turner, James Morton, 'Digging Tunnels, Building an Identity: Sandhogs in New York City, 1874–1906', *New York History*, Vol. 80, No. 1, January 1999, pp.29–70.

On *Empress of Ireland*

Côté, Samuel, *À la découverte de l'Empress of Ireland – 1964*, Quebec, Les éditions GID, 2022.

Creighton, David, *Losing the Empress: A Personal Journey*, Toronto, Dundurn Press, 2000.

Croall, James, *Fourteen Minutes: The Last Voyage of the Empress of Ireland*, London, Stein and Day, 1979.

Dubé, Langis, *Mes 369 plongées sur l'Empress of Ireland*, Quebec, Les éditions GID, 2022.

Grout, Derek, *Empress of Ireland: The Story of an Edwardian Liner*, Toronto, Tempus Publishing Ltd, 2002.

——, *RMS Empress of Ireland: Pride of the Canadian Pacific's Atlantic Fleet*, Stroud, The History Press, 2014.

Kinder, Ian, *A Tale of Two Sisters: The History of the Atlantic Empresses*, self-published, 2014.

——, *The 96th Voyage: The Truth About the Empress of Ireland Tragedy*, self-published, 2017.

McMurray, Kevin, *Dark Descent: Diving and the Deadly Allure of the Empress of Ireland*, Toronto, McGraw-Hill, 2004.

Michel, André, *Histoire d'eau, Empress of Ireland*, Mont-Saint-Hilaire, Musée des Beaux-Arts de Mont-Saint-Hilaire, 2016.

Renaud, Anne, *Into the Mist*, Toronto, Dundurn Press, 2010.

Saint-Pierre, David, *L'Empress of Ireland, une histoire par l'image*, Québec, Les éditions GID, 2016.

Wood, Herbert P., *Till We Meet Again: The Sinking of the Empress of Ireland*, Toronto, Image Publishing, 1982.

Zeni, David, *Forgotten Empress*, Devon, Halsgrove, 1998.

Other Works

Bardon, Michael F.; Galen R., Perras; & J. Graham Lindsay, *Robert Owen King: Engineer, Scientist and Inventor*, self-published, Blurb.ca, 2023.

Desgagnés, Hubert, *C'était en 1914, l'année des charbonniers, Naufrage du C.G.S. Montmagny, le 18 septembre 1914*, Self-published, 2014.

Dansereau, Bernard, *L'avènement de la linotype: le cas de Montréal à la fin du XIXe siècle*, Montreal, VLB, 1992.

Elgar, Francis (dir.), *Fairfield Shipbuilding and Engineering Works*, London, Engineering, 1909.

Fitch, Tad, & Michael Poirier, *Into the Danger Zone: The Lusitania, First Battle of the Atlantic, and Liners During the Great War*, self-published, Blurb, 2014.

Henderson, Bruce B., *True North: Peary, Cook and the Race to the Pole*, New York, W.W. Norton & Co., 2005.

Homer, A.N., *The Imperial Highway*, London, Causton, 1911.

Innis, Harold A., *A History of the Canadian Pacific Railway*, Toronto, McLelland, 1923.

Marcil, Eileen Reid, *Au rythme des marées: l'histoire des chantiers maritimes Davie*, Toronto, McClelland & Stewart, 1997.

——, *Shipbuilding at Québec, 1763–1893: The Square Rigger Trade*, PhD dissertation, 1987.

Oliff, Richard, *Fastest to Canada: The Royal Edward from Govan to Gallipoli*, Silver Link, 2004.

Phillips, John L., *The Bends: Compressed Air in the History of Science, Diving, and Engineering*, New Haven, Yale. University Press, 1998.

Saward, Joe, *The Man Who Caught Crippen*, Southam, Morienval Press, 2010.

Talbot, Frederic A., *The Canadian Pacific Railway*, London, A. & C. Black Limited, 1915.

Walker, Alastair, *Four Thousand Lives Lost: The Inquiries of Lord Mersey Into the Sinking of the Titanic, the Empress of Ireland, the Falaba and the Lusitania*, Stroud, The History Press, 2012.

Walker, Fred M., *Ships and Four Thousand Lives Lost Shipbuilders: Pioneers of Design and Construction*, Barnsley, Seaforth Publishing, 2010.

Winklareth, Robert J., *Naval Shipbuilders of the World: From the Age of Sail to the Present Day*, London, Bloomsbury Academic, 2000.

The numerous large compressors necessary to pressurise the inside of the ship, pushing out the river water and making the hull float. (Ralph S. Blydenburgh photo album, author's collection)

Ralph Stratton Blydenburgh strikes a pose on the refloated SS *Gut Heil*, 1917. (Ralph S. Blydenburgh photo album, author's collection)